101
AMAZING THINGS
about CAT LOVERS

Todd Hafer

BroadStreet
PUBLISHING

BroadStreet Publishing Group, LLC
Racine, Wisconsin, USA
BroadStreetPublishing.com

IOI AMAZING THINGS ABOUT CAT LOVERS

ISBN-13: 978-1-4245-5261-0 (hardcover)
ISBN-13: 978-1-4245-5262-7 (e-book)

Published in association with MacGregor Literary, Inc.

Stock or custom editions of BroadStreet Publishing titles may be purchased in bulk for educational, business, ministry, fundraising, or sales promotional use. For information, please e-mail info@broadstreetpublishing.com.

Art direction by Garborg Design Works
Interior by Katherine Lloyd at theDESKonline.com

Printed in China
16 17 18 19 20 5 4 3 2

Contents

	Introduction..	7
1	You're an Ailurophile (Probably)..................................	9
2	All the President's Cats	10
3	To the Cats Go the Spoils	11
4	Thank You, Mr. Lowe..	13
5	Cats in Need of a Home...	14
6	One Smart Cat..	15
7	Play It Again, Nora...	16
8	You're Too Kind ... No, Seriously—*Way* Too Kind!...........	17
9	A Most Useful Gift?..	19
10	Busted for Cat Possession	20
11	Cat Law...	21
12	A Walk on the Wild Side?...	22
13	Walk Like an Egyptian	23
14	Sir Winston and Jock	25
15	Before You Kiss Your Cat	26
16	Who Are You Callin' Stupid!?.....................................	27
17	Aunt Harriet's Cat	28
18	A Cat Is a Life-Saver!..	29
19	Great Minds Think Alike	31
20	It's Good to Be the Queen . . . of Cats.........................	32
21	Cat-Napped!	33
22	Cats Have the Write Stuff!	35
23	Cat Sparks Genius...	36

24	The Original Cat Lady?	38
25	The Beatle and the Cat	40
26	The Cat Co-Star	41
27	The Presidential Gift-Cat	42
28	The Nightingale Who Loved Cats	44
29	Don't Hold the Tardar Sauce	45
30	You Can't Catch Cooties from Your Cat	46
31	Why Boxes Rock	47
32	Going Green with Your Cat	49
33	Cat Inns Are In!	52
34	A Home for Fast Cats	53
35	Towser the Mouser	54
36	The Angel of Men and Cats	56
37	The Scaredy-Cat	57
38	The Truth Behind Mr. Bigglesworth	58
39	From the Streets to the White House	60
40	Cat Love versus Dog Love	61
41	A Sisterhood of Cats	63
42	Calvin the Cat-Lover	64
43	That Famous Cartoon Cat	65
44	"Let Them Have Cats!"	66
45	"I Simply Can't Resist a Cat."	68
46	Who's Allergic to Whom?	69
47	An Actress "Gone" on Cats	70
48	Man of Crime . . . and Cats	71
49	Hold That Tiger, Mister President!	73
50	The Secrets of Cat Comforting	74
51	Who Were the True Pet Pioneers?	75

52 A Nerd and His Cats 77

53 Presidential Cats . . . and Rats, and Gators? 78

54 One Clean Cat 80

55 Can You Taste That Smell? 81

56 Spy Cats 83

57 Bible Cats? 84

58 Tony and Snow 85

59 Do You Know Cat CPR? 87

60 The Old Man and His Cats 88

61 Cheetahs: One Fast Pet! 89

62 What Makes Luna Tick? 92

63 Do You, Barbarella, Take These Cats 93

64 Catnip: Not Just for Cats 94

65 Cocteau: One Cool Cat 95

66 Sir Isaac and Spithead 97

67 Maru Loves a Box—and Internet Fame 98

68 Bukowski on Cats 100

69 The Feline, Feminine Mystique 101

70 Recession-Proof Pets 102

71 Cat People versus Dog People 104

72 Atchoum Is Nothing to Sneeze At! 106

73 All in the Family? 107

74 "Call Me Crookshanks . . . or Pumpkin." 109

75 Is Your Ragdoll Really a *Ragdoll*? 110

76 Fit to Be Feline 114

77 To Declaw or Not to Declaw? 115

78 Calvin and Hobbes: More Than the Sum of Their Parts 115

79 All Hail Morris! 117

80   China versus Egypt versus . . . Cyprus? 119

81   Ke$ha Says, "Cats Rock!" 120

82   Is Your Cat a Show-Off? 122

83   Talk to the Tail! 123

84   Quoth the Cat 124

85   Lucky Lindy's Cat 125

86   The Silent Meow 127

87   Franco Loves Felines...128

88   A Dog-Like Cat? 129

89   The Blessing of Barney 131

90   Your Feline Favors Classical Music (Probably) 132

91   The Mystery of the Purr..134

92   Tidy Drinkers 135

93   A Foster Parent for Cats 137

94   So Hard to Say Goodbye...138

95   The Queen of the "Crazy Cat Ladies?" 140

96   The Right Pedigree 141

97   Cat Fight! 142

98   Cats on Broadway...144

99   A Tale of Two (or More) Kitties..147

100   Cats Are Family..148

101   Looking for Kitty Convicts 150

ABOUT THE AUTHOR 153

PARTIAL BIBLIOGRAPHY 155

Introduction

Cats. They were worshiped in ancient Egypt and persecuted in medieval Europe. In the thirteenth century, Pope Gregory IX, who viewed cats as "familiars of witches" and minions of the dark side, launched a seek-and-destroy mission that terrorized cats and their owners for almost five hundred years.

Indeed, one of Gregory's successors, Pope Innocent VIII, had cats burned, right alongside their owners.

But, as any cat person knows, felines are survivors. Today, they are America's favorite pet, more than ninety million strong. More than one-third of American households boast at least one feline friend.

We love our cats for myriad reasons. They are loving, mysterious, playful, and loyal. They accept us, quirks and all, and expect that we will do the same for them. They connect with us emotionally, often without making a sound.

Inside this book's covers, you'll discover truly amazing things about cats and the people who love them. Which US President is the No. 1 Cat Fan of all? Why should cats and their owners enjoy catnip together? Who is the great poet who said, "When my cats aren't happy, I'm not happy"? And why should you thank a cat for your wireless Internet connection?

There are at least 101 intriguing things to discover about America's most popular pet. So curl up with your cat and let some remarkable cats and their "people" walk their way into your heart.

And who knows—maybe you'll find yourself loving your cat (or cats) even more. If that's even possible.

1

YOU'RE AN AILUROPHILE
(PROBABLY)

Are you an ailurophile? Because you are reading this book, you probably are. Don't worry. You are not alone. America is full of them. An ailurophile is someone who loves cats, and Americans really, really love their cats. In fact, 67 percent of the country's 90 million cats get to sleep with their owners. Seventy percent of these folks bestow cat birthday gifts. Almost 40 percent of felines get a Christmas present. All told, the average cat owner spends more than $1,000 annually on each furry friend. And 60 percent of cat-owning families include their felines in family photos.

By the way, according to some animal behaviorists, if your cat loves you back, he or she will gaze at you through half-closed eyes. (This, however, is probably not a sign of affection from your human significant other.)

Did You Know?
A cat's tongue feels scratchy because it is covered with tiny rear-facing barbs, perfect for grooming itself, or tearing meat from a bone. And, of course, giving a tickling kiss to its owner.

A generous person will prosper;
whoever refreshes others will be refreshed.

PROVERBS 11:25

2

ALL THE PRESIDENT'S CATS

Abraham Lincoln was a standard-setter on many fronts. Few people know that Honest Abe was the first president to have pet felines at the White House. His wife, Mary Todd Lincoln, was once asked, "Does the President have any hobbies?"

She responded, "Yes—acquiring and caring for cats." Lincoln loved cats and would play with them, and the family dog, Fido, for hours. A favorite feline was son Tad's cat Tabby, whom Lincoln fed with a gold fork at White House dinners. During the Civil War, while visiting General Ulysses S. Grant's headquarters, Lincoln rescued three freezing kittens from a telegraph hut. He tucked them into his coat and brought them to the White House to join Tabby and Dixie (who were both gifts from Secretary of State William H. Seward).

The president once said of Dixie, "She is smarter than my whole Cabinet. And furthermore, she doesn't talk back!"

Speaking of Cats (and Dogs) . . .

"I care not much for a man's religion on
whose dog and cat are not the better for it."

Abraham Lincoln

Therefore, as God's chosen people, holy and dearly loved,
clothe yourselves with compassion, kindness, humility,
gentleness and patience.

COLOSSIANS 3:12

3

TO THE CATS GO THE SPOILS

If you think you spoil your cat, consider the ancient Egyptians.
This culture revered cats more than any in history. Cats got to
wear bling such as golden collars, earrings, and nose rings. At meal
time, they shared plates with their owners. (And we're not talking
about left-overs here. Cats dined at the table.) Even in times of
famine and poverty, household felines were well fed and cared for,
including being anointed with scented oils. They were bathed and
groomed regularly. Some talented owners composed hymns that

praised feline beauty and grace. Not surprisingly, cats held a higher place in most Egyptian households than most of the humans.

In ancient Egypt, housecats were valued for more than their charming companionship. They were able killers of scorpions and snakes that would invade homes. And they protected grain from mice and rats. They even protected books from being gnawed on.

Did You Know?

A cat's front claws stay sharp because they are retracted into their skin pockets when the cat walks or runs. The claws on the hind feet do not retract, so they are usually worn down.

Spread your protection over them,
that those who love your name may rejoice in you.

PSALM 5:11

4

THANK YOU, MR. LOWE

If you are a cat-owner, you should give thanks for Edward Lowe. You probably don't recognize the name; few people do. However, what Lowe did in 1947 would change cat ownership forever. He developed the first commercially packaged cat litter. His litter was simple: pelletized clay that absorbed liquids and odors. (Before he came up with cat litter, Lowe sold clay to garage owners to soak up oil and gas spills.) Today's litters are fancier and more expensive—featuring pine sawdust, wheat husks, or silica gel pearls—but they do basically the same thing.

From those simple clay pellets grew an industry that is worth more than $1 billion today—and worth every penny!

Speaking of Cats . . .

"What's the best cat litter?
Any kind that my cat will actually use!"
Marcia Edwards

For we are to be to God
the pleasing aroma of Christ. . . .
2 CORINTHIANS 2:15

5

CATS IN NEED OF A HOME

While most cats have adoring owners, an estimated 60 million feral (or never-owned) cats roam the United States. These cats gather around a food source, such as a Dumpster behind a restaurant or a college cafeteria. Fortunately, volunteers (many of whom are cat owners), animal shelters, and organizations like the Humane Society work to identify colonies and give the feral cats the care and attention they need. You can help prevent this problem by supporting your local animal shelter, advocating responsible pet ownership in your community, or joining the Humane Society. (Visit hsus.org for more information.) The Humane Society is our nation's largest animal-protection organization, working to improve the lives of cats and other animals at home and abroad.

Did You Know?

Cats are said to have nine lives because the cat-goddess Bast had nine souls, just like her counterpart, the "sun god" Ra. Incidentally, because they love to bask in the sunlight, cats were called "children of Ra" by the ancient Egyptians. And Ra was nicknamed the Tomcat and was sometimes drawn as a wildcat.

As you enter the home, give it your greeting.

MATTHEW 10:12

ONE SMART CAT

As many cat owners know, felines are better pupils than many people think. Animal behaviorist Robert Dollwet (known on the Internet as Catmantoo) adopted Didga the Wondercat from an animal shelter and proceeded to explode old myths about recalcitrant kitties. Dollwet has shown thousands of people that cats can be trained, via positive reinforcement. Didga can surf, skateboard, play dead, follow directional commands, swim, and somersault. Didga can also navigate obstacles on a "Purr-kour" course and stop on a dime—literally. Just visit YouTube to see what we mean.

Did You Know?

Cats can be trained to walk on a leash. However, you should never use a dog collar for your cat. Its neck and spinal anatomy differ from a dog's, requiring a custom harness.

A man's wisdom illumines him
and causes his stern face to beam.

ECCLESIASTES 8:1 NASB

PLAY IT AGAIN, NORA

When Betsy Alexander and Burnell Yow adopted Nora, a gray tabby, from a New Jersey animal shelter, they didn't know they were bringing home a musical prodigy. Alexander is a piano teacher, and Nora loved to sit near the piano when she gave lessons. One day, Nora decided to try her paws at the keyboard. She leaped onto the piano bench. The rest is Internet history. Nora, whose musical style has been described as "scattered, staccato jazz," is an Internet sensation. Her debut YouTube performance garnered more than fourteen million views, and subsequent videos have been popular as well. She also has her own website and blog.

"I didn't teach her," Alexander confesses. "If I could, wouldn't all seven of my cats be playing? What a hit that would be on YouTube!"

When she first discovered Nora's talent, Alexander sought answers from her local veterinary office. "I told them, 'She's playing the piano—what do you think?' Alexander recalls. "They said, 'We don't know.'"

One animal behaviorist has theorized that Nora started playing the piano because she craved the attention Alexander was giving her students.

In 2009, Nora was named Cat of the Year by the ASPCA. "Nora may not be a traditional hero," explained the ASPCA's Jo Sullivan, "but she is an amazing representation of what's in shelters today. This is not a damaged animal. She's an amazing animal. She's an amazing and dedicated creator."

These words, no doubt, were music to Nora's (and her owners') ears.

> *Did You Know?*
> Cats can make about 100 different sounds—and that's without a piano. A dog can make only about 10 sounds.

The LORD is my strength and my shield;
My heart trusts in Him, and I am helped;
Therefore my heart exults, And with my song
I shall thank Him.

PSALM 28:7 NASB

8

YOU'RE TOO KIND ...
NO, SERIOUSLY—WAY TOO KIND!

Animal protection officers in Halland County, Sweden, were forced to confiscate two cats from their owners. The reason: Excessive coddling. The two women owners pushed their "babies" in strollers and, when mealtime came, strapped the cats into high chairs to spoon-feed them. Both cats were also encouraged to suck on pacifiers, and one woman (allegedly) attempted to nurse the cats. (All suspects are innocent until proven otherwise.)

Reporting on the incident, Swedish public broadcast network SVT noted that the cats had to be removed from their owners because they "were not being allowed to develop natural animal behavior."

Speaking of Cats . . .

"My husband and I have found a great system
for cleaning the litter box: Neither one of us does it."

Constance Rivers

The sleep of a laborer is sweet,
whether they eat little or much, but as for the rich,
their abundance permits them no sleep.

ECCLESIASTES 5:12

A MOST USEFUL GIFT?

In the year 884, the Japanese emperor Koko was given a cat as a gift, courtesy of the nation of China. As we have already learned in this book, cats were prized for their rodent-catching ability. However, Koko was so enamored of his feline present that he thought rat-wrangling was beneath its dignity—as well as that of the other cats who arrived in his country. Instead, Koko filled Japan's cities, granaries, and silkworm farms with statues and paintings of cats, the feline equivalent of scarecrows. Scare-cats?

Unfortunately, the rats showed little regard for images of cats. Japan endured heavy economic losses for hundreds of years, especially in the once-lucrative silkworm industry. Finally, in 1620, cat-loving Japan allowed cats to hunt freely.

Speaking of Cats

"There are two means of refuge
from the miseries of life: music and cats."

Albert Schweitzer

Each of you must bring a gift in proportion
to the way the LORD your God has blessed you.

DEUTERONOMY 16:17

10

BUSTED FOR CAT POSSESSION

Some people love their cats so much that it's almost criminal. However, in fifteenth-century Europe, cats and their owners found themselves open to prosecution, courtesy of the powerful Catholic church. The fact that cats are active at night, intelligent, and resistant to human subjugation led some Catholic authorities to conclude that cats were accomplices of the devil. It didn't help matters that a few cat-worshiping cults emerged at this time. (One such cult, known as Freya, featured a pagan goddess who drove a chariot pulled by cats.) This superstition and fear led to the killing of both cats and their owners. Some cat owners were burned as witches.

Sadly, the destruction of millions of cats probably led to the Great Plague, which claimed the lives of twenty-five million Europeans. The Plague, as you probably know, was spread by fleas that were carried along by rats and other rodents. If only the cats had been around to do what they do so well . . .

Speaking of Cats . . .
"If man could be crossed with the cat, it would
improve the man, but it would deteriorate the cat."
Mark Twain

For sin shall no longer be your master,
because you are not under the law, but under grace.

ROMANS 6:14

11

CAT LAW

If TV had been invented in the tenth century, those ubiquitous "Do You Need Legal Help?" ads might have featured Hywel Dda (at least in ads centered on cats). Also known as Hywel the Good, Dda was a Welsh prince and avowed cat lover (although not, officially, a lawyer). He recognized cats' value as both protectors of agriculture and beloved companions. He enacted laws to protect cats, who had been stolen and smuggled for the past one thousand years. He established monetary values for cats and kittens, which laid the groundwork for stiff fines for anyone who harmed or stole a domestic feline.

Under the Law According to Hywel, a kitten was worth a "legal penny," while an adult cat was worth four pence (about $15 in today's money). Of course, as any modern friend-of-felines knows, a cat is priceless. But those fines did significantly reduce cat thefts. And that, Hywel said, is a Good thing.

12

A WALK ON THE WILD SIDE?

The Internet is full of people and their exotic big-cat pets. It might look like an adventure, but in almost all cases, it's better to keep wild cats *wild*. Tigers and lions, and even smaller wildcats like bobcats and ocelots, are dangerous and unpredictable.

For every intriguing YouTube video, there is a horror story, such as the mountain lion, owned by a Texas woman, who mauled her young nephew. Beyond these obvious drawbacks, consider that lions and tigers eat about 40 pounds of meat a day—sometimes downing 100 pounds in a single meal. A lion's weekly food bill can easily approach $4oo. And if you realize that you cannot afford your exotic pet, your local zoo will probably not take them. Most exotic pets end up being euthanized.

Bottom line: Only qualified and well-trained (and rich) professionals should keep wild cats.

> *Did You Know?*
>
> Think your cat sleeps a lot? Wild cats like lions and cougars sleep up to twenty hours a day!

"Is there anyone here who, planning to build a new house, doesn't first sit down and figure the cost so you'll know if you can complete it?"

LUKE 14:28 MSG

13

WALK LIKE AN EGYPTIAN

The ancient Egyptians were ingenious people. They mastered astronomy, surveying, and geometry. They were skilled farmers and warriors. They vanquished many enemies, and enslaved others. But they met their match in one tiny enemy. The rodent. Rodents consumed vast quantities of Egyptian grain, and befouled many more. Pest control became, literally, a life and death matter. The people first turned to the weasel. The weasels ate the rats. And the Egyptians' eggs, chickens, hares—and whatever else they could sink their teeth into. Further, the weasels were untamable, smelly, and uninterested in a meaningful relationship with people.

Enter the cat. Intelligent, adaptable, curious, and hungry. A protector and rodent exterminator extraordinaire.

From their artwork, we know the Egyptians prized beauty, grace, strength, and guile. No wonder this was a match for the ages. Soon, the cats themselves became the subject of Egyptian artwork. One painting, circa 3000 B.C.E., shows two kittens. One sits happily on his owner's lap. The other, sporting a silver earring, sits smiling beneath a chair.

Speaking of Cats . . .
"Even a bad day at home with my cat
beats a good day at the office."
Constance Rivers

GOD's angel sets up a circle of protection
around us while we pray.
PSALM 34:7 MSG

SIR WINSTON AND JOCK

Sir Winston Churchill was many things. A statesman, a leader, an author, and a cat lover. Churchill owned many cats. One of his favorites was Nelson, named after the British admiral. The Prime Minister once boasted, "Nelson is the bravest cat I ever knew. I once saw him chase a huge dog out of the Admiralty. I decided to adopt him and name him after our great admiral."

Churchill's marmalade cat, Jock, often slept with his master and shared his place at the dinner table. Jock was by Churchill's side for his eighty-eighth birthday celebration. Churchill adored the cat, even though he shredded furniture and carpeting while sharpening his claws. If Jock was ever late for dinner, Churchill would send servants to fetch him. He declined to eat until Jock was present. Jock was with the Prime Minister on his deathbed, comforting him till the very end.

Did You Know?

According to a Hebrew legend, Noah prayed to God, seeking protection for all the food he had stored on his ark. He feared the rats and mice would eat it all. In reply, God made one of the lions sneeze—and out popped a cat. "Problem solved!" God declared. "You're welcome."

By faith Noah, when warned about things not yet seen,
in holy fear built an ark to save his family.

HEBREWS 11:7

15

BEFORE YOU KISS YOUR CAT . . .

As we have already learned, Americans love their cats—all 90 million-plus of them. However, among the many ways to show your feline affection, smooching him or her is not the best idea. Don't believe the adage that a cat's or dog's mouth is cleaner than a human's. Yes, the average human mouth harbors about 37 types of bacteria, but a dog's has 53 and a cat's has 130!

So, the next time you want to show your cat some love, try a cuddle, a tummy rub, or a few tender caresses.

To be fair, however, consider this list of things that probably harbor more germs than your cat's mouth:

1. Your kitchen sponge.
2. The bottom of your purse (or gym bag)
3. Your paper currency
4. Your phone
5. The handrails in your home.
6. Your TV remote (and especially the one at hotels)
7. The bedcovers at hotels.

Create in me a pure heart, O God,
and renew a steadfast spirit within me.

PSALM 51:10

16

WHO ARE YOU CALLIN' STUPID!?

On the cat intelligence scale rankings, Persians score relatively low, receiving four out of a possible ten points, according to an Animal Planet study. (Also ranking low are the Exotic Short-hair and Himalayan—both derived from the Persian.)

Of course, Persians' owners are likely to take exception to the low score. Here's a piece of evidence to use in rebuttal: A Persian named Cuty Boy is, unofficially, the Smartest Cat in the World. Cuty Boy made headlines (and YouTube) for his ability to communicate with humans, solve math problems, and understand multiple languages.

To paraphrase Forrest Gump, "Smart is as smart does."

Speaking of Cats . . .

"When you tell a cat what to do,
there's always a question of will he or won't he."

George Burns (on his pet cat Willie)

You will keep in perfect peace those whose minds
are steadfast, because they trust in you.

ISAIAH 26:3

17

AUNT HARRIET'S CAT

Harriet Beecher Stowe, the famed author of *Uncle Tom's Cabin*, had a ghost-writer, of sorts. Stowe's assertive Maltese cat, Calvin, often sat on her shoulder while she wrote. Calvin, whom Stowe named after her husband, walked into her home one day "out of the great unknown." Stowe was deeply attached to the feline Calvin, so she was disheartened when a family move meant she had to leave him behind. She gifted the cat to her dear friend and fellow writer Charles Dudley Warner.

Warner warmed to Calvin as well. The cat became the star of Warner's famous essay "Calvin: A Study in Character."

"Long life to you! Good health to you and your household! And good health to all that is yours!"

1 SAMUEL 25:6

18

A CAT IS A LIFE–SAVER!

In 2012, Wisconsin resident Amy Jung and son Ethan stopped at their local Humane Society to play with the cats. A twenty-one-pound orange-and-white feline named Pudding captured their attention—and their hearts. Jung learned that the cat had been in and out of the shelter for several years, so she decided to adopt Pudding, and his buddy, Wimsy.

Back at home hours later, Jung suffered a diabetic seizure while sleeping in bed. Pudding sprang into action. He sat on his new owner's chest, trying to wake her. When that didn't work, the resourceful cat nudged and nipped at her face until she became conscious. Jung called out to Ethan, but he was asleep and didn't hear her. Pudding was on the case again. He sprinted to Ethan's room and pounced on his bed, alerting him to the crisis. Ethan awoke and called 911.

Jung told her local paper that she wouldn't have lived through the night without Pudding. Her doctors shared her belief.

Eventually, Pudding was registered as a therapy animal, as he learned to sit by Jung's feet and meow whenever he senses that his diabetic human's blood sugar is low.

Speaking of Cats . . .

"The cat is witty, he has nerve,
he knows how to do precisely the right thing
at the right moment. He extricates himself from
the most difficult situation by a little pirouette."

Henri Poincare

The LORD will rescue his servants;
no one who takes refuge in him will be condemned.

PSALM 34:22

19

GREAT MINDS THINK ALIKE

Yes, cats' brains are relatively small, composing just 0.9 percent of their body mass. But, according to "Psychology Today" magazine, "The brains of cats have an amazing surface folding and a structure that is about 90 percent similar to ours [humans']." The cerebral cortex, the brain region responsible for processing information, is more complex in cats than in dogs. Furthermore, a cat brain boasts 300 million neurons. A dog's? One hundred and sixty million. Dog lovers boast that canines are smarter than felines, but now "cat people" have ammo to refute this claim.

Here's one more cat fact for your arsenal. In 2010, a sophisticated super-computer performed 83 times slower than a cat's brain!

Did You Know?

While cats are smart like their owners, they share other, less desirable traits as well. An estimated 55 percent of American cats (almost 50 million of them) are overweight or obese.

ᴖᴖ

Finally, brothers and sisters, whatever is true,
whatever is noble, whatever is right, whatever is pure,
whatever is lovely, whatever is admirable—if anything
is excellent or praiseworthy—think about such things.

PHILIPPIANS 4:8

20

IT'S GOOD TO BE THE QUEEN . . .
OF CATS

Queen Victoria is known for many things (including the tradition of brides wearing white for their weddings). Further, when US President Abraham Lincoln was assassinated, the queen set the standard for reaching out to someone in grief. A widow herself, Her Majesty wrote a touching letter to Mary Todd Lincoln. She included these words:

"I earnestly pray that you may be supported by Him to whom Alone the sorely stricken can look for comfort in this hour of heavy affliction."

She signed the letter, "I remain, dear Madam, your sincere friend Victoria."

It's no surprise that a woman with such a tender heart was a cat lover. In fact, Queen Victoria was instrumental in restoring the domestic cat to its former glory (after years of being maligned as a minion of the dark side). The queen loved her cats (and dogs too), and, through her example and her words, she helped rebuild the domestic cat's sterling reputation as a playful, loving, and clever companion.

At a large bazaar, she made a show of buying two pairs of Siamese cats. On a trip to Wales, her traveling companions included two Persian kittens, whom she rarely allowed out of her sight. *The London Times* noted, "The Queen has done much to make cats popular pets of society."

British aristocracy has boasted many cat lovers, including Princess Victoria, Lady Decies, the Duchess of Bedford, and Lady Colin Campbell. But they all follow in the royal footsteps of Victoria.

Speaking of Cats . . .

"As every cat owner knows, nobody owns a cat."
Ellen Perry Berkeley

For the Lord comforts his people
and will have compassion on his afflicted ones.

ISAIAH 49:13

21

CAT-NAPPED!

While modern tales of cat-thefts are rare, cat-napping was a very real concern to the ancient Egyptians. By 900 B.C.E., cats had become an integral part of Egyptian life. As we learned earlier in this book, cats were prized for being saviors of the land's agricultural riches, as well as for their delightful companionship. Egypt had no desire to share their feline secret with the rest of the world. Thus, exporting cats was illegal. And punishable by death.

Enter some opportunistic and death-defying smugglers. These criminals began swiping cats from their owners and transporting them far and wide—to Italy, Greece, Asia, and beyond. Wherever food supplies—and books!—were threatened by rats and mice, cats were in demand. Ironically, while the Greeks and Romans admired cats' utilitarian value, it took hundreds of years before these countries warmed up to cats the way the Egyptians did.

Speaking of Cats . . .

"A cat will be your friend if he deems you worthy of friendship, but not your slave!"

Theophile Gautier

The day of the Lord will come
like a thief in the night.

I THESSALONIANS 5:2

22

CATS HAVE THE WRITE STUFF!

Louisa May Alcott, author of the classic *Little Women*, was once asked if she had any vices. She responded, "My inordinate love of cats." Alcott's fondness for felines echoed in her writing. In *Little Women*, which is based on the author's life, the March sisters adore their pet cat and her kittens.

The book includes a poem titled "A Lament for S. B. Pat Paw," which eulogizes a beloved pet cat. Alcott writes,

> "We mourn the loss of our little pet,
> And sigh o'er her hapless fate,
> For never more by the fire she'll sit,
> Nor play by the old green gate."

Did You Know?

The muscular Maine Coon cat is one of America's oldest breeds. It was exhibited at agricultural fairs as early as 1860, the year before Abraham Lincoln took office as president (and eight years before *Little Women* was first published.

This cat is, possibly, descended from Norwegian Forest Cats, which sailors brought to America, where it bred with local cats. (For another theory on the ancestry of the official feline of the state of Maine, keep reading this book!)

Fix these words of mine in your hearts and minds. . . .
Teach them to your children, talking about them when
you sit at home and when you walk along the road. . . .
Write them on the doorframes of your
houses and on your gates. . . .

DEUTERONOMY 11:18-20

23

CAT SPARKS GENIUS

Nikola Tesla will go down in history as one of the world's keenest scientific minds. He's the man behind alternating electrical current, the radio (years before Marconi), the laser, robotics, the electric motor, wireless communication, the drone, X-rays, radar, and, of course, the Tesla coil. He even won a few technical debates with Thomas Edison. He spoke eight languages and had a photographic memory.

On the personal side, his life was less electric. He was an obsessive hand-washer, and, for reasons unknown, he despised round objects. And he was, reportedly, celibate until the day he died at age eighty-six.

But he did love animals. He loved his childhood cat Macak, whom he called "the finest of all cats in the world." Macak was more than a companion to young Tesla. One night, he petted Macak and noted the "shower of sparks" of static electricity his affection produced. His mother told him to stop petting the cat, fearing her son would "start a fire." But this early "experiment" with electricity would keep Tesla mesmerized for more than eighty years. One wonders how all of our lives would be different today, if not for a young Serb's childhood pet.

Later in life, however, Tesla found a new favorite animal: the pigeon. Especially one particular pet pigeon. When it died, the scientist wrote, "Yes, I loved her as a man loves a woman . . . and she loved me. When that pigeon died, something went out of my life. . . . I knew my life's work was over."

There is no evidence that a cat had anything to do with the pigeon's demise. However, we all know how jealous a cat can be. . . .

Speaking of Cats . . .

"I was the happiest [boy] of all, the fountain of my enjoyment being our magnificent Macak, the finest of all cats in the world. I wish I could give you an adequate idea of the affection that existed between us. We lived for one another. Wherever I went, Macak followed, because of our mutual love and the desire to protect me."

Nikola Tesla

Those who are wise will shine like the brightness
of the heavens, and those who lead many to righteousness,
like the stars for ever and ever.

DANIEL 12:3

24

THE ORIGINAL CAT LADY?

C olette, the French novelist and actress, has been described as "the original Cat Lady." The author of *Gigi* (and the woman who discovered Audrey Hepburn) loved cats all of her life. In fact, one of her novels is titled *The Cat*. It centers on a couple who is divided over the husband's hapless devotion to his cat, Saha.

This husband, Alain, sounds like he is channeling his author when he says, "It wasn't just a little cat I was carrying at that moment. It was the incarnate nobility of the whole cat race . . . her tact, her bond of union with the human aristocrat."

Who but a true cat lover could put those words into the mouth of a character?

Speaking of Cats . . .

"There are no ordinary cats."

Colette

"Remember, LORD, how I have walked before you faithfully and with wholehearted devotion and have done what is good in your eyes."

ISAIAH 38:3

Top 10 Least Popular Biblical Names for a Cat

10. Ananias
9. Sapphira
8. Pontius
7. Kevin
6. Methuselah
5. Jehoshaphat
4. Jezebel
3. Bathsheba
2. Mephibosheth
1. Judas

(Honorable Mention: Whore of Babylon, Herod, James the Lesser, Bildad the Shuhite, and Tricia.)

25

THE BEATLE AND THE CAT

Count John Lennon among the many music artists who loved cats. As a little boy, he would bicycle to the fishmongers to buy hake for his cat.

One day while the then-famous Lennon was working in the recording studio, a receptionist brought in a litter of kittens. The receptionist recalled, "John immediately knew what I was thinking and said, 'No, we can't. We're traveling too much.' I picked up a black kitten and put him over my shoulder. John rolled his eyes and said, 'Now you've done it! Now you've done it!'

"I wondered what I'd done. John came over and started petting the kitten. He said, 'Well, I guess we have to have a cat.' At the end of the day, John asked if there were any more [kittens] left. I went back and got the only [other] kitten that remained—a white one that no one wanted, because she was so loud. John christened the two kittens Major and Minor. He loved those cats. They reminded him of his days with his Aunt Mimi, whom he playfully referred to as the Cat Woman."

Lennon and his first wife, Cynthia, owned up to ten cats at a time. One of them was named Mimi.

Speaking of Cats . . .

"Cat lovers turn into cat collectors."

Greg Kinnear

May God give you heaven's dew and earth's richness—
an abundance of grain and new wine.

GENESIS 27:28

26

THE CAT CO-STAR

The 1974 film *Harry and Tonto* portrays the story of a seventy-two-year-old man who is forced from his New York apartment, so he decides to pack his pet cat, Tonto, in a carrying case and hit the road. The philosophical Harry was played by Art Carney. Tonto the cat played himself. Carney (of *The Honeymooners* fame) confessed that he did not like cats before the movie. However, during the filming, Tonto won him over.

Thus, Carney is utterly believable when his character is told he cannot take Tonto on an airplane. He calmly declines boarding the plane and takes a bus instead.

Despite having a cat as his major co-star, Carney won the 1974 Best Actor award for *Harry and Tonto*, the only Oscar of his career. He defeated Albert Finney, Dustin Hoffman, Jack Nicholson, and Al Pacino for the award.

Speaking of Cats . . .

"A man has to work so hard that something of his personality stays alive. A tomcat has it so easy. He has only to spray and his presence is there for years, on rainy days."

Albert Einstein

Two are better than one,
because they have a good return for their labor. . . .

ECCLESIASTES 4:9

27

THE PRESIDENTIAL GIFT-CAT

President Rutherford B. Hayes is not one of the most revered Chief Executives in history, but he can lay claim to being our country's first owner of a Siamese cat. Siam was sent to President Hayes in 1878, as a gift from David Sickels, a US ambassador to Thailand. Siam endured a two-month journey in a Wells Fargo crate from Bangkok to Washington, DC. In a letter trumpeting Siam's arrival, she was described by Sickels as "one of the finest specimens of Siamese cats that I have been able to procure in this country."

The good-natured Siam quickly became a favorite pet of the First Family and their staff. She was allowed to roam the White House at will, and often made grand entrances when the First Lady entertained guests. The President's personal physician, J. H. Baxter, treated and cared for Siam when she became ill with a respiratory infection. After Siam passed away, instructions were given to preserve her, but, despite many searches—including efforts by the Department of Agriculture's museum and the Smithsonian—the preserved Siam has never been located.

Did You Know?

President Thomas Jefferson was thought to own a cat, as White House visitors frequently heard meowing from a nearby room. However, the sounds were from Jefferson's pet mockingbird, Dick, who was adept at mimicking cats, among other animals.

Receiving a gift is like getting a rare gemstone;
any way you look at it, you see beauty refracted.

PROVERBS 17:8 MSG

28

THE NIGHTINGALE WHO LOVED CATS

Florence Nightingale, social reformer and pioneer of modern nursing, was also a devoted cat person. The "Lady with the Lamp" once said, "Cats possess more sympathy and feeling than human beings."

During her lifetime, she owned more than sixty cats—seventeen of them at one time. She took great care of her feline friends. They dined on specially prepared food, served on China plates. Further evidence of Nightingale's bond can be seen on some of her letters, which bear the unmistakable mark of kitten paw prints.

Did You Know?
Jack and Donna Wright of Kingston, Ontario, hold (at press time), the Guinness World Record for owning the most cats, with 689.

Be agreeable, be sympathetic, be loving,
be compassionate, be humble.

I PETER 3:8 MSG

29

DON'T HOLD THE TARDAR SAUCE

Is your cat a budding Internet celebrity? Consider the case of Tardar Sauce, whom you probably know as Grumpy Cat, famous for her sardonic facial expression. Tardar's owner, Tabatha Bundesen, didn't know she was living with a famous feline, whose "resting grump face" is due to an underbite and feline dwarfism.

Then, about five years ago, her brother posted a picture on the social-news website Reddit. More photos, with captions, followed. The "Official Grumpy Cat Page" was launched on Facebook. It garnered more than eight million likes. A grumpy star was born. Grumpy Cat was featured on the front page of the *Wall Street Journal* and the cover of *New York* magazine. Bundesen quit her job at Red Lobster to focus on Grumpy's burgeoning career.

Bundesen seems to have made the right move. Yes, Grumpy might miss those Red Lobster leftovers, but she isn't crying in her water bowl. Her fame continues to grow. At press time, Grumpy was scheduled to be honored with her own animatronic waxwork at Madame Tussaud's museum in San Francisco.

Speaking of (Grumpy) Cats . . .
"My house is run, essentially, by an adopted, fully clawed cat with a mean nature."
Anthony Bourdain

"The LORD does not look at the things people look at.
People look at the outward appearance,
but the LORD looks at the heart."
1 Samuel 16:7

30

YOU CAN'T CATCH COOTIES
FROM YOUR CAT

Cooties, that mysterious "condition" that has hampered many a schoolyard romance, are real. Cooties are lice, parasitic insects who like to dwell on humans and many other warm-blooded creatures—including your pet cat or dog.

Body lice are the brand that are commonly called cooties, and they are truly to be feared by children and adults alike. They can spread typhus fever. However, you do not need to fear procuring lice from your cat, and vice versa. Lice are species-specific. A brand of lice called Felicolasubrostrata is the only kind that infests cats.

Incidentally, the term cootie might spring from the Malay word kutu, which means "biting insect."

And so the word of the Lord [regarding salvation]
was being spread through the entire region.

ACTS 13:49 AMP

31

WHY BOXES ROCK

Pet stores and the Internet abound with clever cat toys, but some savvy pet owners believe that nothing makes a cat purr like the simple box. As any cat knows, a box is more than a container. It's a hiding place, a comfort zone, and the cardboard equivalent of a security blanket.

A study conducted at a Dutch animal shelter found that providing "hiding boxes" for newly arrived cats lowered their stress levels, helped them adjust to their new surroundings faster, and made them more interested in interacting with humans.

This comfort-seeking behavior can be seen throughout the

feline world. Wild cats seek retreat in tree tops, dens, and caves. House cats find the same in that shoe box from Zappos. Why? To quote from *The Domestic Cat: The Biology of Its Behaviour:* "Cats do not appear to develop conflict resolution strategies to the extent that more gregarious species do, so they may attempt to circumvent antagonistic encounters by avoiding others or decreasing their activity." Translation: Your cat would rather hide than fight.

Here's another reason why boxes rock a cat's world. According to a study by the National Research Council, the thermoneutral zone for a domestic cat is 86 to 97 degrees Fahrenheit. So, set your thermostat to a toasty 91 degrees or so and your cat is comfortable because it doesn't have to generate extra heat to keep warm—or expend metabolic energy to cool off. However, this Cat Comfort Zone is about 20 degrees higher than humans'. That's why you can find your fuzzy friend sprawled near a large window and soaking up the sunlight. Or sitting on your computer keyboard.

That's also why many cats enjoy curling up in cardboard boxes, including some that seem disproportionately small. Corrugated cardboard is a great insulator, and a small box induces a cat to ball up, preserving maximum body heat.

So there it is: A box is an insulated and stress-busting comfort zone. It's a safe place where a feline can hide, relax, sleep, and plot its next mission. A box can be the ultimate cat toy, and it's free. Of course, you don't have to reveal this fact to your cat.

Did You Know?

The heaviest cat on record is Himmy, a Tabby from Queensland, Australia. He weighed almost 47 pounds, and lived to be 10 years old. He probably tried to wedge himself into a shoebox on more than one occasion.

You are my hiding place; you will protect me
from trouble and surround me with songs of deliverance.

PSALM 32:7

32

GOING GREEN WITH YOUR CAT

Most pet owners are cautious with household cleaners and candles, but many common houseplants and produce are toxic or irritating to cats. From avocados and eggplant to honeysuckle and tiger lilies, the list of toxic plants is longer than most people think. For a complete list, visit the Humane Society's website (hsus.org) or ask for a list from your veterinarian. This will help you know which flora to avoid, or to place in a cat-free zone of your home.

"Many plants, both in the house and the yard, can be toxic to our pets," says Dr. Tina Wismer, D.V.M. "Some toxic plants cause only mild stomach upset, but others can be poisonous. As a pet owner, it's important that you be familiar with the most dangerous of the toxic plants—like Sago Palms, Easter lilies, Japanese yews, and azaleas."

Did You Know?

The world rarest coffee, Kopi Luwak, comes from Indonesia, home to a wild cat known as the luwak. This cat eats coffee berries, and the beans inside the berries pass through the cat's stomach. The beans are then harvested from the cat's scat and cleaned and roasted. Kopi Luwak sells for $500 for a one-pound bag. If you can find it being served at a coffee shop, a cup of Kopi will dent your bank account for $35 to $80.

He makes grass grow for the cattle,
and plants for people to cultivate—
bringing forth food from the earth. . . .

PSALM 104:14

Cat-Safe Greenery

Here is one list of cat-safe plants. For a more complete list, ask your vet or visit a trusted website, such as the Humane Society's (hsus.org) or the American Society for the Prevention of Cruelty to Animals (aspca.org).

Alfalfa sprouts
Areca palm
Baby rubber plant
Begonia
Catmint
Chamomile
Dahlia
Lemon button fern
Oregano
Ponytail palm
Sage
Spider plant
Thyme
Zinnia

33

CAT INNS ARE IN!

The traditional hotel-chain industry is facing challenges, but specialized pet hotels are booming. The dog-spa chain Dogtopia now boasts more than twenty-five locations. The luxury D Pet hotels have opened in trendy Hollywood, Scottsdale, and Manhattan. Pets R Inn has locations in five states.

What makes a pet hotel different from a mere pet-friendly hotel?

Well, at the Holiday Pet Barn resorts in Virginia, cats enjoy "furrmazing" multi-level condos, with special features such as a private hidden potty, a built-in aquarium with moving fish, and a state-of-the-art ventilation system. At these resorts, your cat will also receive a "Compawssion Hug" twice a day.

Out West, in Washington state, the Canine Country Club and Cattery features cat condos separated from the canine rooms. And the Cattery offers a jungle-gym scratching post and a window with a "beautiful landscaping view" in every room.

It seems we humans may economize on many leisure expenses, but not on the comfort of our four-footed friends.

Did You Know?

According to one survey (by the American Pet Products Manufacturers Association) 29 percent of single-cat households and 43 percent of multiple-cat households consist of cat who showed up on a doorstep or wandered into a yard. Indeed, as cat owner Marcia Edwards says, "We don't choose our cats; our cats choose us!"

The fear of the LORD leads to life;
then one rests content, untouched by trouble.

PROVERBS 19:23

34

A HOME FOR FAST CATS

Olympic sprinter Carmelita Jeter is not the only fast one in her home. Jeter owns five rescue cats—Sticks, Tye, Iverson, Casper, and Tango. The quintet loves to race around her home. "They constantly run around the house, chasing each other, as if they are in a track meet," the world champ says. "It's really cute."

She and her cats have been featured in *Cat Fancy* magazine.

At press time, Jeter was training for the 2016 Olympics, hoping for more world records and gold medals. However, if she raced her cats, she might actually lose. A fit cat hit speeds of 31 miles per hour, and that's faster than even Carmelita "The Jet."

Seen in a Church Bulletin:
Next week's "Bring Your Cat to Church Day" has been cancelled, due to an outbreak of common sense.

Do you not know that in a race all the runners run,
but only one gets the prize?
Run in such a way as to get the prize.

I CORINTHIANS 9:24

35

TOWSER THE MOUSER

Think your cat is a good mouser? Before you answer, consider the prowess of Towser the Mouser, a tortoise-shell moggy, who lived to be almost twenty-four. During her lifetime, she caught 28,899 mice—along with assorted rats, rabbits, and other critters. Towser was the official mouser for the Glenturret

Distillery in Crieff, Scotland. (Mice love to feast on barley and can quickly overrun a distillery if they are not stopped.)

For almost a quarter-century, Towser caught an average of three mice a day, earning a place in the *Guinness Book of World Records* as the best mouser on the planet. The distillery applauded her by featuring her paw prints on the label of Fairlie's Light Highland Liqueur.

Today, a statue stands in her honor at the distillery site. Its inscription reads:

Towser
21 April 1963—30 March 1987
Towser, the famous cat who lived in the still house,
Glenturret Distillery, for almost 24 years.
She caught 28,899 mice in her lifetime.
World mousing champion, *Guinness Book of Records*

Did You Know?

One study of house cats who foraged for their own food found that mice made up 90 percent of their diets.

ᴗᴖ

"Well done, good and faithful servant!
You have been faithful with a few things;
I will put you in charge of many things."

MATTHEW 25:23

THE ANGEL OF MEN AND CATS

It's natural that a woman as compassionate as Clara Barton was a cat-lover. Barton was a schoolteacher who, after the Civil War began, became a nurse who served on the front lines, tending to soldiers even as bullets flew by her. She was fearless in her work, as her father had convinced her that serving on the battlefield was her Christian duty. For her efforts, she earned the nickname "Angel of the Battlefield." Her selfless attitude is reflected in one of her most famous quotes: "Would that Christ would teach my soul a prayer that would plead to the Father for grace sufficient for you. God pity and strengthen you, every one."

After the war, Barton founded the American Red Cross and worked with President Abraham Lincoln (another cat person) to locate and provide proper burials for tens of thousands of Union soldiers.

In appreciation for Barton's selfless work, US Senator Schuler Colfax once gave her a kitten. Barton's favorite cat was Tommy, the black-and-white who kept her company for seventeen years. A portrait of Tommy, painted by Barton's friend and fellow nurse Antoinette Margot, is still displayed in the Barton house in Glen Echo, Maryland.

In all their distress he too was distressed,
and the angel of his presence saved them. In his love
and mercy he redeemed them; he lifted them up. . . .

ISAIAH 63:9

37

THE SCAREDY-CAT

No one crafts conflict quite like legendary scare-meister author Stephen King, the man behind *The Shining*, *The Stand*, and *Pet Sematary* (which featured one scary cat on its cover). "It might be," he once wrote, "that the biggest division in the world isn't between men and women but [between] folks who like cats and folks who like dogs."

King does not take sides in this age-old debate. His family has kept cats and dogs as pets. In one photo, one of King's cats sports a name tag that reads "Clovis." Clovis, as King fans know, is the name of the heroic cat in the author's screenplay for *Sleepwalkers*.

Speaking of Cats . . .

"Cats were the gangsters of the animal world, living outside the law and often dying there. There were a great many of them who never grew old by the fire."

Stephen King

The LORD is my light and my salvation—
whom shall I fear?

PSALM 27:1

38

THE TRUTH
BEHIND MR. BIGGLESWORTH

Mr. Bigglesworth, the bald pet cat of Douglas Powers in the *Austin Powers* movie franchise, was originally a long-haired cat, like the Turkish Angora favored by infamous James Bond villain Ernst Stavro Blofeld. However, according

o the Powers legend, Mr. B. lost his luxurious fur in a cryo-
genic capsule.

In real life, Mr. Bigglesworth goes by the moniker Ted Nude-
Gent. He's a champion purebred Egyptian Sphinx cat, bred by
Michelle Berge of California's Belfry Cattery. Ted's casting was
ideal, for more reasons than his lack of follicles. Sphinx cats are
very sociable and easy to train. Series star Mike Myers can con-
firm this fact, as Ted grew very fond of the actor during filming.
He would often climb onto Myers' lap to take a nap.

Incidentally, the character Mini-Me's cat, "Mini Mr. Bigglesworth," was played by three Sphinx kittens, whose real names
are Mel Gibskin, Paul Nudeman, and Skindiana Jones.

Did You Know?

Actress Tippi Hedren (*The Birds*) owned a kitten
named Marlon Brando.

Indeed, the very hairs of your
head are all numbered.

LUKE 12:7

FROM THE STREETS
TO THE WHITE HOUSE

Perhaps the most famous White House pet of all time is Socks the Cat, a stray who was adopted by Chelsea Clinton when her father, Bill, was governor of Arkansas. The black-and-white feline was a fixture at the White House during the eight years of the Clinton presidency. He was often photographed on the Chief Executive's shoulder (despite his reported cat allergy) and was generally given free reign of the country's most famous residence. Socks showed up often in photos of the Oval Office and the White House's press-briefing room.

Socks also boasted his own online fan club and appeared at many animal-charity events. He was the co-star of Hillary Clinton's book *Dear Socks, Dear Buddy: Kids' Letters to the First Pets*.

When the Clinton family left the White House in early 2001, Socks stayed in Washington, DC, moving in with Betty Currie, the President's longtime secretary. The Clintons visited him many times when they traveled to DC. Socks lived for 20 years, and when he passed away in 2009, many major news outlets published his obituary.

Speaking of Cats . . .

"Socks brought much happiness to Chelsea and us
over the years, and enjoyment to kids and cat lovers
everywhere. We're grateful for those memories. . . ."

Bill and Hillary Clinton

I tell you, use worldly wealth to
gain friends for yourselves, so that when it is gone,
you will be welcomed into eternal dwellings.

LUKE 16:9

40

CAT LOVE VERSUS DOG LOVE

It's a debate that seems as old as time: Who loves their humans more, cats or dogs? The answer: Both. Here's the scoop: According to a study conducted at London's Lincoln University, your cat loves you and needs you—but not in the same way a dog does. "Although our cats were more vocal when the owners rather than a stranger left them [as part of the study]," said the study's authors, "we didn't see any additional evidence to suggest the bond between a cat and its owner is one of secure attachment."

The people behind the study are quick to point out that thi does not mean that cats don't develop close relationships with their owners. They do. It simply means that the bonds cats form are not based on the dog-like need for security. This is likely because cats are independent hunters who are not as thoroughly domesticated as dogs. While we humans bred dogs to fit our needs, cats, essentially, moved in with us because the perks were good. Scientists have concluded that, even after thousands of years of living with people, cats remain only "semi-domesticated."

Moreover, cats and dogs have different social structures. House cats "are not pack animals," notes Celia Haddon, author of *Cats Behaving Badly* and *How to Read Your Cat's Mind*. "So they are not going to depend on their owners. But it doesn't mean that they don't want to be around their owners. This study shows that they really do."

Did You Know?

Biologically speaking, your cat's brain is more similar to yours than it is to a dog brain. Humans and cats share nearly identical brain regions that are responsible for emotions.

�

"I truly understand that God shows no partiality,
but in every nation anyone who fears him
and does what is right is acceptable to him."

ACTS 10:34-35 NRSV

A SISTERHOOD OF CATS

The talented Bronte sisters shared more than a love of writing. They loved cats. Felines play starring roles in many of the sisters' writing, including *Agnes Grey* (by Anne) and *Wuthering Heights* (by Emily). The diaries of Anne and Charlotte also proclaim the family love of cats.

In her essay "Le Chat" (French for "The Cat") Emily defends cats against those who argue that they are selfish or mean-spirited. Emily notes that cats' dispositions are very similar to humans, and she argues that "the cat's self-reliance is much better than the hypocrisy of humans."

Emily admiringly added, "A cat is an animal who has more human feelings than almost any other being. A cat, in its own interest, sometimes hides its misanthropy under the guise of amiable gentleness; instead of tearing what it desires from its master's hand, it approaches with a caressing air, rubs its pretty little head against him, and advances a paw whose touch is soft as down."

Speaking of Cats . . .

"She [the cat] was trusted and valued
by her father, loved and courted by all dogs, cats,
children, and poor people, and slighted
and neglected by everybody else."

Anne Bronte

An honest answer is like a kiss on the lips.

PROVERBS 24:26

42

CALVIN THE CAT—LOVER

President Calvin Coolidge's affection for cats was no political ploy, designed to win the appeal of the cat-loving constituency. Coolidge was a cat fan from way back. As a young Vermont farmboy, he saved a litter of kittens from drowning. Cats had always been part of his life, so it was no surprise that our 30th president owned several cats in the White House. Their names Smokie, Blackie, Tiger, Bounder, Timmie, and Climber (a Turkish Angora whom Coolidge nicknamed Mud).

The presidential pet repertoire also featured larger cats—a bobcat and two lion cubs.

Timmie, incidentally, regularly bunked with the Coolidge family canary, Caruso, one of several uncaged birds the family owned. The two pets usually snoozed together at night.

Tiger, a gray-striped American shorthair, could often be found walking beside the President or wrapped around his neck. Once, when Tiger wandered away from home, Coolidge pleaded for his safe return during a national radio address. The cat was eturned and fitted with a special collar that included his contact nformation, including the famous White House address.

> *Did You Know?*
> Seventy percent of Americans include their pets' names on their greeting cards.

Whoever seeks good finds favor. . . .

PROVERBS 11:27

43

THAT FAMOUS CARTOON CAT

J im Davis grew up on a farm with twenty-five cats. That's not a staggering fact, but consider the way these cats inspired this cartoonist from Muncie, Indiana. In the late 1970s, Davis was surveying the American newspaper comics scene and noting that dogs ruled—Snoopy, Marmaduke, Fred Basset, and all the rest. "Where are the cats?" Davis wondered. In 1978, he began publishing "Garfield," a comic featuring a lazy, lasagna-loving cat, based on those farm cats he grew up with. The cat shared the name (and some of the personality traits) of Davis's grandpa,

James A. Garfield Davis, whom the grandson described as " large, cantankerous man." Presumably, he hated Mondays.

Today, "Garfield" has been syndicated in more than 2,50 newspapers and other publications worldwide. It is the world most widely syndicated strip, and Garfield merchandise racks u about $1 billion every year. Apparently, Davis's hopes to create " marketable character" have been realized.

Speaking of Cats . . .

"Love me, feed me, never leave me."
Garfield the Cat

"This is the bread that came down from heaven.
Your ancestors ate manna and died,
but whoever feeds on this bread will live forever."
JOHN 6:58

44

"LET THEM HAVE CATS!"

arie Antoinette married at fifteen and assumed the role (a nineteen) as France's queen. Her lavish lifestyle earned he the nickname "Madame Deficit," from her disloyal subjects, an her infamous line about the peasants, "Let them eat cake!" didn't do much for her popularity either.

But her cats, several Persians and Angoras, loved her, and she loved them. (Her husband, Louis XVI, however, hated them and often tried to use them for target practice.)

After Louis and Marie's two decades on the throne came the French Revolution. The monarchy crumbled, and Marie's hubby was guillotined (in January of 1793). A few months later, Madame Deficit met the same end.

Her cats, however, met a better fate, at least according to some legends. Some of Marie's possessions were smuggled by royalist sympathizers onto a trading ship (the Sally), which was headed for Maine. The sympathizers had hoped to place Marie on the vessel, but they were not able to rescue her from prison in time. Among the rescued possessions, some believe, were the queen's cats. Once in America, the new cats on the block bred with the locals, and the Maine coon cat was the result. Can these large, long-haired, and bushy-tailed critters truly trace their origins to Palace of Versailles? That's a matter of some dispute, but few people have come up with a better explanation.

Did You Know?

In ancient Egypt, wealthy families treated their cats like royalty. When cats died, they were mummified. As a sign of mourning, the owners shaved off their eyebrows and continued to mourn until those eyebrows grew back. Cats were so special that anyone who killed one, even by accident, was sentenced to death.

The Lord will rescue me from every evil attack
and will bring me safely to his heavenly kingdom.

2 TIMOTHY 4:18

45

"I SIMPLY CAN'T RESIST A CAT."

Mark Twain (born Samuel Clemens) was dubbed "the father of American literature" by William Faulkner. He was also a father to many cats during his lifetime. He kept eleven cats at his farm in Connecticut. "I simply can't resist a cat," he wrote, "especially a purring one. They are the cleanest, cunningest, and most intelligent things you know, outside of the girl you love, of course."

Twain is also famous for the quote, "If you hold a cat by the tail, you learn things you cannot learn any other way."

Despite that tongue-in-cheek quote, the man behind Tom Sawyer and Huck Finn adored his cats. He would command them, "Come up," and they would join him on his chair. He could tell them, "Go to sleep," and they would (usually) obey. In several photos from late in his life, a cat is perched on his shoulder or on his lap. When he played pool, he sometimes let a cat watch from the corner pocket, where it would occasionally paw at a passing ball.

. . . .

Speaking of Cats . . .

"When a man loves cats, I am his friend and comrade,
without further introduction."

Mark Twain

And this is love: that we walk in obedience to
his commands. As you have heard from the beginning,
his command is that you walk in love.

2 JOHN 1:6

46

WHO'S ALLERGIC TO WHOM?

While 10 percent to 30 percent of Americans are allergic to cats (depending on which allergist you believe), did you know that cats can be allergic to people—sort of? According to one study, feline asthma, which affects one in two hundred cats, is on the rise. And human lifestyle is to blame. Because cats are more frequently kept indoors, they are more susceptible than ever to inflammation of their airways caused by cigarette smoke, dust, human dandruff, pollen, and even some brands of cat litter!

So if your cat is wheezing and sneezing, you might be to blame. In rare cases, a cat can even catch the flu from its owner.

> **Did You Know?**
> Chocolate contains a substance called theobromine, which is poisonous to cats. And it is even more toxic to dogs.

I live and breathe God.

PSALM 34:2 MSG

47

AN ACTRESS "GONE" ON CATS

The English actress Vivien Leigh (of *Gone with the Wind* fame), owned many cats during her life. She was especially fond of Siamese cats. She once said, "Once you have kept a Siamese cat, you would never have any other kind." Leigh's first Siamese, New Boy, was a gift from husband Laurence Oliver. New Boy sported a custom collar imported from Paris. The cat can be seen in many photographs with the actress.

After New Boy passed away, Leigh adopted Poo Jones, a seal-point Siamese. Poo and Leigh traveled the world. He had his own luggage and often napped in Leigh's dressing room while she was onstage or in front of the movie cameras.

> **Did You Know?**
> The year 1985 marked the time when cats eclipsed dogs as America's most popular house pets.

Keep traveling steadily along his pathway and
in due season he will honor you with every blessing....

PSALM 37:34 TLB

48

MAN OF CRIME . . . AND CATS

Author Raymond Chandler was one of those few success stories that emerged from the Great Depression. The Chicago-born Chandler decided to try his hand at writing after he was fired from his oil company job during the Depression.

At age forty-four, he began writing for magazines. He published his first novel, *The Big Sleep*, in 1939, at age fifty-one. That novel introduced his signature character, detective Philip Marlowe, who would be featured in books and film. In addition to writing novels, Chandler also wrote the screenplays for *Double Indemnity* and *The Blue Dahlia*. He earned Academy Award nominations for both films.

Chandler was an avid cat fan. He often wrote about his cats. He even wrote *as* his cat, Taki. Here's an example of Chandler's/Taki's work, as the cat addresses a feline companion: "Come around sometime when your face is clean, and we shall discuss the state of the world, the foolishness of humans, the prevalence of horse meat, although we prefer the tenderloin side of a porterhouse, and our common difficulty in getting doors opened at the right time and meals served at more frequent intervals. I have got my staff up to five a day, but there is still room for improvement."

Speaking of Cats . . .

"A cat never behaves as if you were the only bright spot in an otherwise clouded existence. This is another way of saying that a cat is not a sentimentalist, but that does not mean that it has no affection."

Raymond Chandler

God can testify how I long for all of you
with the affection of Christ Jesus.

PHILIPPIANS 1:8

49

HOLD THAT TIGER, MISTER PRESIDENT!

United States presidents have received several unusual gifts over the centuries, but perhaps Martin Van Buren (1837-1841) has a leg up (or paw up) on his competition. The Chief Executive once received a pair of tiger cubs from the Sultan of Oman.

The president was, reportedly, enamored with the cubs. Congress, however, was less enthralled. They deemed that perhaps the White House was not a good home for two growing apex predators. They pressured Van Buren to make the Executive Mansion a tiger-free zone. The president decided not to be catty about the matter. "They belong to the people," he said of the tigers, and he donated them to a local zoo.

Did You Know?

About 15 percent of American households regularly feed a stray cat. (This is a kind gesture, but it has its downfalls, such as adding to the cat overpopulation problem or bringing disease to one's "official" pets.) Many veterinarians suggest either adopting a cat full-time or notifying a local shelter.

"If the home is deserving, let your peace rest on it. . . ."

MATTHEW 10:13

50

THE SECRETS OF CAT COMFORTING

What cat-lover doesn't long to comfort his or her pet when it's scared or in distress? However, we humans should remember that our pets want a different kind of comfort than we do. According to a study at England's University of Lincoln, "If a cat is scared or has been involved in an incident, it's not going to want a cuddle."

According to Alice Potter, one of the study's authors, a cat in crisis "is going to want to withdraw or hide, so owners need to provide a place for that to happen." (As we have learned earlier, a box is a great cat refuge.)

The findings of the British study are important, because a survey by Cats Protection, a pet-welfare charity, revealed that more than 50 percent of cat owners said they would calm their pets by cuddling them—the opposite of what a frazzled feline wants and needs.

Potter adds, "We hope this study will help cat owners better understand their pets."

Did You Know?

According to the market research company WSL, 81 percent of pet owners are spending the same amount of money, if not more, on their pets. According to WSL, "While they cut expenses in other areas of their household budgets, pet owners are still buying monogrammed sweaters, personalized food and water bowls, faux mink coats, and even Halloween costumes for their animals."

You will increase my honor
and comfort me once more.

PSALM 71:21

WHO WERE THE TRUE PET PIONEERS?

As we learned earlier in this book, many scientists believe that cats were first domesticated in ancient Egypt about 4,000 years ago.

However, recent research indicates that one breed of once-wild cats lived near (with?) farmers in China more than 5,300 years ago. "Our data suggests that cats were attracted to ancient

Chinese farming villages by small animals, such as rodents, that were living on the grain that the farmers grew, ate, and stored," says Fiona Marshall, an archaeology professor at Washington University, in St. Louis, Missouri, and one of the people behind this new research. "Results of our study show that the village of Quanhucun was a source of food for the cats 5,300 years ago, and the relationship between humans and cats was commensal, or advantageous for the cats. Even if these cats were not yet domesticated, our evidence confirms that they lived in close proximity to farmers, and that the relationship had mutual benefits."

No matter whom we credit for being the true Cat Pet Pioneers, we can all agree on that part about "mutual benefits."

Speaking of Cats . . .
"My relationship with cats has saved me
from a deadly, pervasive ignorance."
William S. Burroughs

"So the last will be first,
and the first will be last."

MATTHEW 20:16

52

A NERD AND HIS CATS

Neil Gaiman, the author of novels, novellas, graphic novels, and the comic book series The Sandman, might be the coolest nerd on the planet. He describes himself as "a feral child who was raised in libraries," adding, "I was the sort of kid who devoured books, and my happiest times as a boy were when I persuaded my parents to drop me off in the local library on their way to work, and I spent the day there."

Gaiman grew up reading the works of cat lovers like Edgar Allen Poe, and today he owns several cats. He often chronicles some of their adventures on his blog, which boasts more than 1 million readers. (He also has more than 1.5 million followers on Twitter.)

Many of Gaiman's fans have thrilled to the adventures of the felines Coconut, Hermione, Pod, Zoe, and Princess. He describes that last cat this way: "I've grown so used to having a bad-tempered but beautiful cat that I need to warn visitors about. She's outlasted all the cats I loved and all the cats I bonded with. And I think she's grown very used to me."

He continues, "When Zoe died, it was really easy to explain to people how much you could miss a sweet, gentle cat who was nothing but a ball of utter love. I'm going to have a much harder time one day, months or even years from now, explaining why I miss the meanest, grumpiest, and most dangerous cat I've ever encountered."

> *Speaking of Cats . . .*
>
> "The cat dropped the rat between its two front paws.
> 'There are those,' it said with a sigh . . . 'who have
> suggested that the tendency of a cat to play with
> its prey is a merciful one—after all, it permits the
> occasional little running snack to escape, from time to
> time. How often does your dinner get to escape?'"
>
> *Neil Gaiman (from the novella* Coraline*)*

Better a patient person than a warrior,
one with self-control than one who takes a city.

PROVERBS 16:32

53

PRESIDENTIAL CATS . . .
AND RATS, AND GATORS?

You've read about some of the US Presidents who welcomed cats to the White House (and you'll read more before we're done), but what's the total tally of Chief Executives who owned a feline?

Thirteen is the number—if you count Martin Van Buren's tiger cubs. And we do.

Incidentally, the White House has been something of a pet menagerie through the years. Beside cats and dogs, Presidential pets include pigs, goats, horses, snakes, rabbits, badgers, cows, fish, geese, guinea pigs, hens, hamsters, roosters, sheep, lizards, a wallaby, a bear, a bobcat, a pigmy hippo, a ram, a flying squirrel, a turkey, a donkey, a raccoon, and a piebald rat. And let's not forget John Q. Adams's pet alligator, which he kept in the White House bathtub.

Among the forty-four presidents, Teddy Roosevelt leads the pet pack, as he had total of twenty-three pets in all. John F. Kennedy ranks a close second with twenty-one. Only Chester A. Arthur and Franklin Pierce failed to own a pet during their White House years.

Another president, Millard Fillmore, didn't have an official pet at 1600 Pennsylvania Avenue, but he was rumored to regularly feed some stray cats, even inviting them into the East Room to sleep on a blanket in inclement weather. Furthermore, he was active in animal protection causes in his home state, New York. He started a branch of the Society for Prevention of Cruelty to Animals in Buffalo. (This organization would eventually become the ASPCA.)

Fillmore explained his love for animals: "When I was a thoughtless boy, I took the life of a mother bird. I remember my father was greatly grieved and said, 'Millard, do you realize what you have done? You have taken the life of a mother, and have left her children to die of starvation in the nest. How would you like to have a great giant come along and kill your father and mother and leave you alone without food or care?' My father's rebuke sank so deeply into my heart that since that day I have never taken the life of a living creature."

Speaking of Cats (and All Animals) . . .

"Becoming involved in animal protection means
being prepared to meet the cold indifference of
the thoughtless multitude, the ridicule and scoffs of
the reckless, and the savage malignity of the cruel.
But it is a good cause."

President Millard Fillmore

I led them with cords of human kindness,
with ties of love.

HOSEA 11:4

54

ONE CLEAN CAT

Have you ever found yourself saying, "If my cat isn't sleeping, it's grooming itself"? You are not alone. According to Cornell University's College of Veterinary Medicine, cats spend up to half of their waking hours cleaning themselves. It's time well-spent. Feline self-cleaning has several benefits. It cools cats off, comforts them, stimulates them, and frees them from odors that might attract predators.

And what about those times the cat turns it grooming prowess on you? According to researchers, that's the feline way of showing you affection and marking you as part of the family. It's the cat's way of saying, "You're my property, and I really like you. Enjoy this cat-bath! You're welcome!"

> *Did You Know?*
> Cats usually groom themselves in the same way, in the same order. Ears, face, top of head, etc. And did you know that when a cat grooms herself, she is also "marking" her fur with the scent of her own saliva. This is why a cat will always groom after being handled or combed or brushed by a human.

Cleanse me With hyssop, and I will be clean;
wash me, and I will be whiter than snow.

PSALM 51:7

55

CAN YOU TASTE THAT SMELL?

You probably know that your cat can see better than you can—especially at night. But did you know that felines outshine humans in the olfactory department as well? Cats possess a vomeronasal organ in the roofs of their mouths. (It's sometimes called a Jacobson's organ.) This olfactory tool allows a cat to literally taste a smell, by keeping its mouth slightly open. (This ability is shared by snakes, lizards, and some other reptiles.) The cat's resulting facial expression, a quasi-grimace, is called flehmen.

This super-smell ability means that your cat can quickly determine if food is fit to eat. And it's why a feline will sometimes walk away from a meal that seems perfectly palatable to its owner. This is also why food straight from the refrigerator sometimes leaves a cat cold. The chill has robbed the food of its enticing odor. (If you suspect this is happening with your cat, a quick spin in the microwave (for the food, not the cat) should do the trick. Besides, room temperature food is easier on a cat's digestive system.

Did You Know?

During his Rough Rider days, President-to-be Teddy Roosevelt adopted a pet cougar for his military unit— as its unofficial mascot.

Christ loved us and gave himself up for us as
a fragrant offering and sacrifice to God.

EPHESIANS 5:2

56

SPY CATS

During the Cold War, the Russians were known for spying on everyone, even the most unlikely victims. In 1961, at the Dutch embassy in Moscow, ambassador Henri Helb was working busily at his desk. Suddenly, his two pet Siamese cats, who had been sleeping nearby, awoke and started pawing at an office wall. At first, Helb thought his pets heard a mouse scurrying about inside the wall. However, when he bent close to the wall, he could hear nothing. He decided further investigation was warranted.

Inside the wall, he discovered a hidden microphone, which had been switched on remotely, using radio waves. The cats, with their super-powered hearing, could hear the microphone, which had been installed by Russian spies, when it turned on.

Thanks to these alert cats, the embassy staff began misleading the Soviets, conducting fake "top secret" meetings, always held near the microphone. They proceeded to provide Russian spies with loads of worthless information, enough to keep them spinning their wheels and wasting time and money for quite a while.

Did You Know?

Cats' dish-shaped ears, with their large echo chambers, give them ultrasonic hearing ability. Some cats can detect frequencies as high as 100,000 hertz (though the average is about 65,000 hertz). A dog's range is 35,000 to 40,000. Humans rank a distant third in the auditory department, maxing out at about 20,000 hertz. In fact, if you are reading this book by lamplight, your cat can probably hear the electricity flowing through the power cord right now!

Apply your heart to instruction
and your ears to words of knowledge.

PROVERBS 23:12

57

BIBLE CATS?

While house cats are not mentioned in the Bible (like their relatives the lion, tiger, and panther), feline-themed legends and fables abound. One of the best known centers on mice, which, according to the legend, were created by the devil, in order to destroy the earth's crops, and, in turn, doom all of humankind

When He saw the devil's plot unfolding, God created cats, who could keep the devil's rodents in check. From that day on, cats have been true friends, companions, and helpers of people.

Speaking of Cats (and all creation) . . .
"God sets out the entire creation as a science class-room, using birds and beasts to teach wisdom."

Proverbs 35:11 MSG

58

TONY AND SNOW

Rescuing a cat from the ocean while in Montenegro came naturally for Tony Azevedo. First, he is a cat person. Second, as an elite water polo player, aqua rescue was right in his wheel-house. Azevedo named the all-white rescue cat, whom some children had tossed in the water, Snow.

As human and feline bonded, Azevedo discovered that Snow loves to chew on wet hair. It was a match made in cat heaven. How many cat owners spend most of their workday in the water?

Azevedo adds, "Snow loves to watch me cook at night when I come home from practice. Then, once I've eaten and settled onto the couch to unwind before bed, she climbs right up on me to snuggle. It's our nightly routine."

As this book went to press, Azevedo (who was born in Brazil but is an American citizen), was training for the 2016 Olympic Games, his fifth straight Olympics. But whatever the outcome, Snow will always think her life-saver of an owner is as good as gold.

Did You Know?

Female cats, like Snow, tend to be right-pawed, while male cats usually favor the left paw. Conversely, 90 percent of humans are right-handed, and the 10 percent of us who are lefties tend to be male. (In one study, 11.6 percent of men were lefties, compared to 8.6 percent of women.)

For it is by grace you have been saved,
through faith—and this is not from yourselves,
it is the gift of God,

EPHESIANS 2:8

59

DO YOU KNOW CAT CPR?

M ost responsible cat owners take their pets to a vet regularly. Some even have a Cat First Aid Kit. But what if your cat was having a breathing or heart problem? Is there such a thing as Cat CPR?

Yes. Did you know that the American Red Cross conducts pet CPR classes? Dr. Deborah Mandell helped update the organization's course materials, and she hopes many pet owners will get up to speed on this life-saving procedure. Mandell works in the emergency room at the University of Pennsylvania's Matthew J. Ryan Veterinary Hospital, so she knows that pet CPR works.

"I have definitely seen patients whose owners have performed CPR at home or in the car and have saved their pets," Mandell reports. "so I am a huge advocate, obviously, of having all pet owners know it."

Indeed, more than sixty percent of vet visits are emergencies, according to the American Animal Hospital Association (AAHA). For more information on pet CPR, consult your veterinarian, the American Red Cross, or websites like aaha.org or vetstreet.com.

Did You Know?

The American Veterinary Medical Association (AVMA) now recommends acupuncture for many feline pain-related problems, including arthritis, joint disease, and epilepsy.

Above all else, guard your heart,
for everything you do flows from it.

PROVERBS 4:23

THE OLD MAN AND HIS CATS

Some would say that a hard-living man like Ernest Hemingway would not be a cat person. Some would be wrong.

Hemingway, author of classics like *The Old Man and the Sea*, *A Farewell to Arms*, and *For Whom the Bell Tolls*, shared his Key West home with as many as thirty cats, including Snowball, a six-toed feline given to him by a ship's captain. (Some of Snowball's alleged descendants still roam Papa Hemingway's former home—now a museum—in Key West. The six-toed cats among them are sometimes called Hemingway Cats.)

The World War I vet and Nobel Prize winner for literature had already accumulated twenty-three cats by the 1940s. He referred to them as "purr factories" and "love sponges." There are many photos of Hemingway and his cats, at his writing desk—and on the dinner table.

Speaking of Cats . . .

"A cat has absolute emotional honesty. Human beings, for one reason or another, may hide their feelings, but a cat does not."

Ernest Hemingway

Rescue me from my enemies, Lord,
for I hide myself in you.

PSALM 143:9

CHEETAHS: ONE FAST PET!

In the 1920s and '30s, American celebrities like Phyllis Gordon and Josephine Baker traveled with them as pets. But today, times have changed and cheetahs are no longer legal to have as American house pets. Is this law a good one?

It depends on whom you ask. Cheetahs can be tamed, somewhat. Domestication of these fast cats dates back to 1,200 B.C.E. Egypt, when the Egyptians tamed and trained cheetahs to assist them on hunts. More recently, South Africans Hein and Kim Schoeman adopted two cheetah cubs and raised them along with their two children (ages three and one), recording their experiences in a documentary titled *Cheetah House*. In the documentary, the cheetahs can be seen playing fetch, riding shotgun on car rides, and hanging out with the toddlers.

Additionally, cheetahs are legal pets (and status symbols) in the United Arab Emirates, in some West Asian countries, and parts of Africa. With a technique known as "affection training," cheetahs can be trained to play fetch and be more comfortable around humans. However, the cats have very specific needs. They need to run regularly, with at least two acres of land at their disposal. They require a carefully monitored diet that includes four pounds of meat daily—including the bones—as well as supplements of vitamins A, D, and E.

Even if you can skillfully train and feed your cheetah, you can't expect it to be domesticated like your pet house cat or dog. "Domestication is a process that takes hundreds of generations of domestication breeding," notes Dr. Laurie Marker, founder of the Cheetah Conservation Fund in Namibia.

So, if you are considering a pet cheetah, the best advice might be, "Not so fast."

> *Did You Know?*
> Unlike a house cat, a cheetah cannot retract its front claws. They act like a track runner's spikes, allowing the big cat to hit speeds of 70 miles per hour.

Come quickly to help me, my Lord and my Savior.

PSALM 38:22

Top 10 Signs
You Are a Cat Person

10. Your morning devotions consist of reading "Garfield" in the funny pages.

9. Your last Christmas letter included the term "ear mites."

8. You win at Scrabble by busting out "Abyssinian."

7. Your family reunions are sponsored by 9Lives.

6. You follow Grumpy Cat on Twitter.

5. Your Visa bill is dominated by purchases of organic catnip and multi-colored cat wigs.

4. You've bid on eBay for a genuine Morris the Cat hairball.

3. For your funeral, you've requested a dramatic reading of "Puss in Boots."

2. You recorded this year's "CFA International Cat Show"—on your wedding DVD.

1. Your ring tone is just a long string of "Meows."

62

WHAT MAKES LUNA TICK?

If Nora the Keyboard Cat [see page 16] ever needs a vocalist, she should call on Luna. Luna is an eleven-month-old rescue cat from Bucharest, Romania, who regularly indulges her owner, Razvan Alexandru, in some delightful duets. In these back-and-forths, Alexandru croons about Luna's beauty and loving nature. Luna responds with simple meows. However, Alexandru translates the true meaning. When he sings, "Come on; let's eat," Luna responds, "Meow-yes."

But when Alexandru sings, "Moony, Moony," Luna responds, "Shut up, you're embarrassing me."

Alexandru seems unfazed by the rebuffs. "She is Luna, the Moon," he says of his pet. "She sings for sailors and lovers. And now she came into my life to sing to me."

Speaking of Cats . . .

"To get a dog to do what you want,
you give it a command. To get a cat to do
what you want, you give it a suggestion."

Bash Dibra

Sing a new song to the Lord!
Sing it everywhere around the world!

PSALM 96:1

63

DO YOU, BARBARELLA, TAKE THESE CATS . . .

After Barbarella Buchner split from her partner of seven years, the forty-eight-year-old feared she would never find love again.

She was wrong. Today, she is married to her two pet tabby cats, Spider and Lugosi—thanks to a website called marryyourpet. com. Buchner, a web designer in England, says she has never been happier. She is so devoted to her feline "husbands" that she has tattooed their initials on her right leg. Her one-bedroom flat in England features more than 350 feline-themed items, including a cat-friendly toilet. She says she has spent "thousands of pounds" on her cats.

"Obviously, I don't have sex with my cats," Buchner explains (needlessly). "There is nothing perverse or disgusting about my union with my cats. Lugosi and Spider have been my constant companions for fourteen years, making it the longest relationship I've ever had with anyone. It's just pure, spiritual, unconditional love on both sides, as simple as that."

She adds, "If Lugosi and Spider died, I would never marry another cat. They are my first cats, and no other cat in the future can change that."

Finally, she has these words for any man hoping to entice her toward human matrimony. "If a man ever approaches me," she explains, "I just tell them straight off: 'Sorry, I'm married to my cats.'"

Did You Know?

The average American household spends more than $1,000 annually on its pet(s). That's more than the amount spent on alcohol, men's clothing, or land-line telephones.

As a bridegroom rejoices over his bride,
so will your God rejoice over you.

ISAIAH 62:5

64

CATNIP: NOT JUST FOR CATS

It makes your cat dance, purr, and tumble, but did you know that catnip (also known as catmint) has many benefits for humans too?

According to websites like herbwisdom.com and organicfacts.net, catnip can nip a variety of digestive problems—from indigestion to diarrhea to gas—in the bud. It even helps ease menstrual cramps.

Catnip infusions and baths are believed to soothe achy muscles, especially those caused by flu or other illness. For many years, catnip's anti-inflammatory properties have made it a popular treatment for arthritis, hemorrhoids, and bug bites. A mild catnip tea might alleviate morning sickness, provide a good night's sleep, and calm frazzled nerves.

Further, catnip can repel certain insects, making it a popular ingredient in some home-made bug repellent.

To find out how a catnip tea, tincture, or bath balm might help you, visit your local natural-foods store, or visit websites like wellnessmama.com, herbwisdom.com, organicfacts.net, and webmd.com.

> *Did You Know?*
> About two-thirds of house cats respond to catnip. Catnip is safe and non-addictive for your cat, but the herb can lose its effectiveness over time if it is used too often.

A cheerful heart is good medicine. . . .

PROVERBS 17:22

65

COCTEAU: ONE COOL CAT

Frenchman Jean Cocteau wore many hats during his life: poet, novelist, filmmaker, playwright, designer, and artist. He earned acclaim for novels like *Les Enfants Terribles* (*The Holy*

. . . .

Terrors) and films like *Beauty and the Beast*. No wonder he was part of an elite social circle that included Pablo Picasso, Coco Chanel, Marlene Dietrich, and Edith Piaf.

He was also a cat devotee who helped found a club in Paris called The Cat Friends Club. The organization, which boasted its own Cocteau-designed membership pin, sponsored cat shows and promoted cat welfare in general.

Cocteau dedicated his illustrated poetry collection "Drole de Ménage" to his cat Karoun, whom he described as "the king of cats."

According to his wishes, Cocteau, who died in 1963, was interred beneath the floor of the Chapelle Saint-Blaise des Simples in Milly-la-Foret, a chapel that dates back to the twelfth century, on the grounds of a former leper colony. His epitaph, located under a picture of the risen Christ, reads, "Je reste avec vous" (I am with you).

Speaking of Cats . . .
"I love cats because I enjoy my home;
and little by little, they become its visible soul."
Jean Cocteau

"And surely I am with you always,
to the very end of the age."
MATTHEW 28:29

66

SIR ISAAC AND SPITHEAD

English physicist and mathematician Sir Isaac Newton is renowned for developing the principles of modern physics and unlocking secrets of motion, mass, and gravity.

Among the keys to Newton's success were . . .

His work ethic ("Genius is patience.")

His humility ("If I have seen further than others, it is by standing upon the shoulders of giants.")

His spiritual nature ("In the absence of any other proof, the thumb alone would convince me of God's existence.")

Newton grew up on a farm, so it's no surprise that he was a cat guy. He was deeply concerned about the welfare of his feline friends. Some biographers speculate that Newton had a mild case of Asperger Syndrome and seemed to get along better with cats than with people. One writer noted, "Cats brought companionship and inspiration to the world's most gifted thinker."

This is no idle speculation. Newton's cat Spithead was responsible for at least one of the genius's inventions. At one point, Newton was experimenting in a pitch-black room, and Spithead kept pushing a door open and compromising the experiment. Newton put his nimble mind to work and invented the cat flap (or cat door). This less-known but much-appreciated invention kept both Newton and Spithead happy. It's done the same for millions of cats and their owners since.

Did You Know?

Here are some facts Sir Isaac Newton could appreciate: All-white cats with blue eyes are often deaf. Furthermore, all-white cats with one blue eye are often deaf on the side with the blue eye.

"To the one who knocks,
the door will be opened."

LUKE 11:10

67

MARU LOVES A BOX—
AND INTERNET FAME

Who is the top cat on the Internet today? It's hard to say, as more and more cats claw for attention, but few would dispute Maru's position as one of the 'Net's favorite felines. At press time, the Scottish Fold, who lives in Japan, has amassed more than 300 million views of his various videos. The average Maru video attracts 800,000 views. His YouTube channel, mugo-mogu, boasts more than a half million subscribers. An article in

London's *The Guardian* ranked Maru as the most popular cat on the Internet, based on views and "how much discussion and creativity" a cat generated. (Tardar Sauce, a.k.a. Grumpy Cat, whom we met earlier, finished second.)

And how many cats can say they have appeared on *Ellen*?

Many of Maru's videos often feature him playing in various boxes. In fact, he launched his career with his now famous "I love a box!" clip. Other videos show Maru playing a tambourine with his tail or simply lounging about the house. His owner, Mugomogu, is almost never seen, although "Maru's Ear Cleaning" is a notable exception.

Unlike some celebrities, Maru has shown himself willing to share the spotlight. A few years ago, Mugomogu adopted a kitten named Hana from a local vet. Will Hana become a 'Net star too?" Only time, and YouTube, will tell.

Speaking of Cats . . .

"I feel at ease with him. No matter how tired I am, as soon as I am with him, he brings a smile to my face. Unfortunately, he refuses hugs, but still. . . ."

Mugomogu (on her pet cat Maru)

When I smiled at them, they scarcely believed it;
the light of my face was precious to them.

JOB 29:24

68

BUKOWSKI ON CATS

Like his fellow writer Ernest Hemingway, Charles Bukowski was a hard-living man whose gritty and whisky-drenched works explored life's darker side. His works include the novel *Barfly* and the poetry collection *Love Is a Dog from Hell*.

But Bukowski also loved himself a cute, cuddly cat. "If you're feeling bad, you just look at the cats," he explained. "You'll feel better because they know everything is, just as it is."

When Bukowski died in 1994, he left behind reams of unpublished material. Some of this was combined to form the poetry anthology *On Cats*. This book reveals the author's love for cats, whom he said were "wise, tough survivors." Furthermore, he said that the company of a cat keeps a person alive longer.

Speaking of Cats . . .

"Authors like cats because they are such quiet, lovable, wise creatures, and cats like authors for the same reasons."

Robertson Davies, novelist

Do not forsake your friend. . . .

PROVERBS 17:10

69

THE FELINE, FEMININE MYSTIQUE

Fans of the classic comic book *Batman* know that Catwoman was a different breed of villain than the Caped Crusader's other foes, like the evil and murderous Joker, Riddler, and Penguin. Batman's creator, Bob Kane, crafted Catwoman as a foil who was not an evil killer. Instead, Catwoman was Batman's occasional love interest as well as his opponent. Kane described her as a "friendly foe who committed crimes but was also a romantic interest in Batman's rather sterile life." Catwoman engaged Batman in a high-stakes chess match as he tried valiantly to reform her.

For Kane, men like Batman resembled dogs, while women were more like the cats he knew. "Women are feline creatures," he explained, "while men were more like dogs. Dogs are faithful and friendly. Cats are cool, detached, and unreliable. Cats are as hard to understand as women are. We [men] don't want anyone taking over our souls, and women have a habit of doing that. So there's a love/resentment thing with women. With women, once the romance is over, somehow they never remain my friends."

Of course, cat devotees would tell Kane that if you've truly won a cat's heart, that romance is never over.

Did You Know?

According to renowned animal trainer Bash Dibra, "A dog responds to his owner's command because he is pack-oriented and considers his owner the leader. A cat doesn't respond to commands, because she doesn't understand them. A cat needs to be shown what is expected of her, or what is not acceptable, in more subtle ways."

In everything set them an example
by doing what is good

TITUS 2:7

70

RECESSION—PROOF PETS

"When my cats aren't happy, I'm not happy."
Percy Bysshe Shelley

According to the American Pet Products Association, pet ownership is one thing that is not trending downward in the tough economy. More than 62 percent of Americans own pets, and we spend big on our pets, recession or no recession. We spent $43.2 billion in 2008, $47.7 billion in 2010, $53 billion in 2012, and $61 billion in 2013. When times are tough, having a cat or dog to cuddle goes a long way. That's one reason why almost 72 million households have a pet—and almost half of all American households have more than one pet.

Pet-services is one growing niche, with more than thirty-five chains providing everything from cat- and doggy-day-care to grooming to dog-walking.

People are willing to cut corners, but not when it comes to pet care. Even picking up after pets has become big business; witness the proliferation of chains like Pet Butler and Wholly Crap. Pet ownership has been increasing by about 4 percent over the past several years, and the trend shows no sign of slowing down.

According to multiple reports, the American population considers their pets to be part of the family. Indeed, almost 70 percent of parents confess that they treat their pets as well as they treat their children. This pet personification means that pet owners purchase holiday gifts, designer outfits, specialty shampoos, and high-tech gadgets like automated food dispensers. As Neva Springston, a longtime cat owner says, "It's not an expense; it's an investment in those we love."

Speaking of Cats . . .

"My cats aren't "just like" members of the family.
They ARE members of the family."
Neva Springston

All honor to God, the God and Father of our
Lord Jesus Christ; for it is his boundless mercy that
has given us the privilege of being born again so that
we are now members of God's own family.

1 PETER 1:3 TLB

CAT PEOPLE
VERSUS DOG PEOPLE

Are you a cat person or a dog person? Even if you answered, "Both," you probably have a preference. As it turns out, dog people and cat people truly do have different personalities, according to recent research. In one study, (conducted with six hundred college students and reported on the website Livescience.com), dog lovers tended to be more energetic and outgoing than cat lovers—and were more likely to follow the rules, rather than deviate from them. Cat lovers were 11 percent more likely to be introverts. They were also more open-minded and more sensitive than their canine-loving counterparts. And cat people tend to be non-conformists.

Another finding is sure to heat up the rivalry among pet owners: Cat owners scored higher in intelligence than dog lovers.

"It makes sense that a dog person is going to be more lively," says psychology professor Denise Guastello, one of the study's authors, "because he or she is going to be outside, talking to people, and bringing their dogs along. Whereas, if you're more introverted and sensitive, maybe you're more often at home, reading a book, because your cat doesn't need to go outside for a walk."

However, no one connected with the survey could offer an explanation for this difference: Dog people usually cite Paul McCartney as their favorite Beatle. Cat lovers tend to prefer George Harrison.

Did You Know?
Snoop Dogg is a cat person. He adores his two Siamese cats, Miles Davis and Frank Sinatra.

Make every effort to keep the unity
of the Spirit through the bond of peace.
EPHESIANS 4:3

72

ATCHOUM IS NOTHING TO SNEEZE AT!

A tchoum is among the felines vying for Internet fame. Atchoum (French for "Sneezy") is, arguably, the first French-Canadian celebrity cat. The exotic Persian hails from Montreal, and his owner, Natalie, is still getting used to the sudden fame. Natalie began posting Instagram and Facebook photos of her cat, with his intense golden eyes and wild fur, in early 2016. They quickly went viral.

Atchoum looks a bit like Albert Einstein on a very bad hair day. The cat has a condition called hypertrichosis, a rare congenital condition that causes excessive hair growth. Atchoum is the first known cat with the condition. There is no cure for hypertrichosis, but its only symptom is excess furriness, which doesn't seem to bother Atchoum or his owner, who happens to be a professional pet groomer.

Explaining her cat's name, Natalie says, "I named him Sneezy, because when you sneeze hard, it messes up your hair and you look like my cat."

On his website, atchoumthecat.com, the cat offers his own perspective. "I'm the hairy but not scary Persian kitten. Some people say my wild furs and intense amber eyes make me look like a dog, an owl, a mad scientist, a Gremlin, Lorax, or the Grinch, but I'm happy to be me. I love life and sharing my adventures every day with you!"

Recently, Atchoum has put his fame to good use. He has teamed with fellow Canadian cat Oreo to "write" a book titled *Atchoum and Oreo: First Day of School*. The story tackles the subject of school bullying and promotes friendship and kindness—and accepting one another's unique traits.

> *Did You Know?*
> All of today's celebrity cats owe a "high-paw" to Felix the Cat. This cartoon cat starred in the first "talkie" cartoon a year before Mickey Mouse. Felix was also the subject of the earliest television test broadcasts in 1928, and he was NBC's official test pattern until the late 1930s.

What matters is . . . your inner disposition.

I PETER 3:4 MSG

73

ALL IN THE FAMILY?

Did you get your pet cat from a friend or relative? According to the American Pet Product Manufacturers Association (APPMA), almost 40 percent of single-cat households got their pet from a friend or relative. This number jumps to more than 52 percent of felines in multiple-cat households.

Friends, family, and pets go together like peanut butter and jelly, marking a longtime American tradition. In 1785, George Washington received pet donkeys as a gift from King Charles III the King of Spain. Abraham Lincoln's dog, Fido, often stayed in Springfield, Illinois, with family, while his president/owner was in Washington, DC. More recently, the Obama family accepted a gift of a puppy, a Portuguese water dog named Bo, from their longtime family friend, the late Senator Edward Kennedy.

However, if you have a neighbor or uncle who regularly tries to gift you with a new kitten (or a donkey), the Humane Society recommends directing the person to a low-cost sterilization clinic (for the animal, not the human).

Did You Know?

In addition to cats and dogs, Abe Lincoln's White House was home to two pet goats, Nanny and Nanko. The president's sons Tad and Willie loved to tie carts or kitchen chairs to the goats and race them around the White House.

Share what you have with others.
God takes particular pleasure in acts of worship—
a different kind of "sacrifice"—that take place
in kitchen and workplace and on the streets.

HEBREWS 13:16 MSG

"CALL ME CROOKSHANKS . . . OR PUMPKIN."

Human actors are praised when they play a person of a different nationality. Pumpkin, a rescue cat from a British animal shelter, took on a more demanding role for the Harry Potter movies. The red tabby Persian played Crookshanks, a half-cat, half-Kneazle hybrid belonging to Hermione Granger (played by Emma Watson). A Kneazle, as Potter fans know, has a lion-like appearance, a firm dislike of shady people, and the innate ability to solve problems.

Pumpkin appeared in the third, fourth, and fifth Potter films. Like a human actor, Pumpkin trained several months for her role. She was calm and well-behaved on the set and followed direction remarkably well. She could sit perfectly still when asked and could run to her mark right on cue. Her only flaw: She was so happy that she purred loudly, forcing the sound crew to adjust their levels accordingly. The cause of all that purring might have been Pumpkin's affection for Watson. The two got along brilliantly.

On the movie set, Pumpkin enjoyed her own dressing room, a stylist, and dinners of roast lamb and chicken. After the last movie wrapped, Pumpkin retired to the Isle of Man with her owner/trainer Donna McCormick-Smith. In retirement, Pumpkin has become something of a diva. She refuses to eat conventional cat food, insisting on roasted meats.

Did You Know?

Crookshanks (played by Pumpkin the Persian) is the only "movie cat" to be featured on a postage stamp. The cat was immortalized on a series of Potter-themed stamps issued by Taiwan in June of 2004.

The wise store up choice food. . . .

PROVERBS 21:20

75

IS YOUR RAGDOLL REALLY A RAGDOLL?

If you've ever referred to your cat as "a ragdoll," make sure you understand your terms. "Ragdoll" is an official cat breed, developed by American breeder Ann Baker in the 1960s. While they are not in the Cat Fanciers Association's top ten breeds, they are well-loved. Ragdolls relax completely when they are picked up. Their spines seem to disappear, and they become limp and pliable like the toy they are named after.

Ragdolls' fur does not have an undercoat, and they shed very little. Their fur does not mat, so these cats require little grooming. They are large, mellow cats who are very affectionate. They love to follow their owners around the house, although they sometimes flop at their humans' feet, meaning that a ragdoll owner must be aware—and nimble. Some of these cats can be taught to fetch and to come when called.

So, now you know the difference between a cat that behaves like a ragdoll and one that is, officially, a Ragdoll!

Speaking of Cats . . .

"I write so much because my cat sits on my lap.
She purrs, so I don't want to get up.
She's so much more calming than my husband."

Author Joyce Carol Oates

Be careful, keep calm and don't be afraid.
Do not lose heart. . . .

ISAIAH 7:4

76

FIT TO BE FELINE

C ats are known for their lounging and grooming, but they enjoy exercise and play as well. However, when picking out a toy to entertain or exercise your cat, choose one best-suited for your cat's personality. If your cat is timid, select a toy that is simple and easy to "conquer." (For example, if a gizmo has a too-big "target toy" on its end, it will look like an intimidating opponent, not a fun item of "prey.") If your feline is confident and athletic, you can choose something more challenging.

Try to make interactive play a regular part of your week. Don't play one day, then take a two-week break. Your cat needs consistency. Make a "play date" once or twice a day. You need only about fifteen minutes per session. You will be surprised what a few minutes of playtime and fun can do for your cat's emotional and physical health—and yours as well.

When playing with your cat, make sure you have all the right moves. Don't wave a toy around frantically. That's not how cats hunt in the wild. Instead, a cat stalks its prey, remaining stealthy and quiet. Move the toy like prey, alternating between fast and slow movement. Let your cat get within striking distance, plan its next move . . . and pounce!

Here's another tip: Movements that go away from or across your cat's field of vision will trigger that predator drive. Don't simply dangle a toy in its face, or "attack" with it.

Hunting is a mental and physical task. Strive to make your feline play time confidence-building, trust-building, and stress-relieving. Your cat must have some successful "captures" or he or she will get frustrated.

Options abound for cat-ercize. If you're a techie, check out games like "Cat Playground" for the iPad. However, if you and your cat are low-tech, there's probably no beating an old tennis ball or ping-pong ball.

Did You Know?

Unsure if your cat is enjoying a game with you? If its whiskers are pointed backward or flattened against its face, your cat is probably annoyed, angry, or afraid.

You will again be happy and
dance merrily with the timbrels.

JEREMIAH 31:4 TLB

77

TO DECLAW
OR NOT TO DECLAW?

Many cat owners face the declawing dilemma, especially after a feline has shredded some furniture or given someone a nasty scratch.

Most veterinarians and animal trainers don't recommend this procedure, which involves intrusive surgery. Declawing includes removing a cat's claws, as well as the toe bones to which the claws are attached. The procedure is usually done only on the front claws, because the rear ones are rarely used for scratching.

Cats can be hospitalized for several days after the procedure, for observation, as infections or other complications can occur. Even after the cat returns home, its paws can remain very sore for several weeks. Many vets recommend replacing standard cat litter with shredded paper during this time.

It should be noted that many breeders insist that potential owners sign an agreement stating they will not declaw their cats. Further, the Humane Society of the United States opposes declawing of cats when done solely for the owner's convenience—without any benefit to the animal.

If you are considering this procedure, consult your veterinarian and/or a trusted animal trainer. Whatever your decision, it should informed and well-considered.

Be sure that everything is done properly
in a good and orderly way.

1 CORINTHIANS 14:40

78

CALVIN AND HOBBES: MORE THAN THE SUM OF THEIR PARTS

"For though there be many things in God's Word
above Reason—that is to say, which cannot by natural
reason be either demonstrated or confuted—
yet there is nothing contrary to it."
Thomas Hobbes

The relationship between humans and their felines has inspired many art forms. However, perhaps no one has tapped into the dynamics of a human/cat interaction like cartoonist Bill Watterson, in his comic strip *Calvin and Hobbes*. The strip enjoyed a ten-year run from 1985 to 1995, and it's been called "the last great newspaper comic." At the apex of its popularity, the strip was featured in more than 2,400 newspapers worldwide. In 2010, reruns of *Calvin and Hobbes* appeared in more than fifty countries. The various *Calvin and Hobbes* book collections have sold more than forty-five million units.

The strip followed the antics of Calvin, an adventurous and precocious boy, and Hobbes, his sardonic stuffed tiger, who is fully alive to Calvin but "just" a stuffed animal to all the other characters. The bond between the two resembles that of many people and their special feline friend. To Calvin, Hobbes is much more than a stuffed pet tiger, and this perspective is one of the strip's defining motifs.

The pair is named after John Calvin, the theologian behind the "Five Points of Calvinism," and Thomas Hobbes, a seventeenth-century political philosopher—the man behind such quotes as "Knowledge is power" and "Ignorance of the law is no excuse."

According to Watterson, the boy and his tiger "are more than the sum of their parts. Each ticks because the other is around to share in the little conspiracies, or to argue with."

Though the series never mentions a specific political figure or current event, it explores a variety of important issues, from environmentalism to public education to the flaws of opinion polls.

Ironically, while this strip was informed by a conservative theologian and a deeply spiritual philosopher (Hobbes said, "Whether men will or not, they must be subject always to the Divine Power. By denying the existence or providence of God, men may shake off their ease, but not their yoke"), Watterson says he has never attended a formal church service.

- -

Did You Know?

"Calvin and Hobbes" was inspired, in part, by another cartoon feline, Krazy Kat. Watterson says that George Herriman's "Krazy Kat," which ran in newspapers from 1913 to 1944, "is the best comic strip ever drawn."

Cause me to understand the way of your precepts,
that I may meditate on your wonderful deeds.

PSALM 119:27

79

ALL HAIL MORRIS!

He was born in 1959 and discovered in 1968 at the Hinsdale Humane Society by animal talent scout Bob Martwick—not long before he was due to be euthanized. Martwick took the fourteen-pound orange tabby home and began to train him. Martwick called his new protégé "the Clark Gable of cats."

One year later, Morris the Cat made his TV debut, playing "the world's most finicky cat," and eating only 9Lives cat food from Purina. Soon, Morris's "signature" appeared on all of the product's packaging.

Morris was a guest at the White House, where he signed,

with President Richard Nixon, the National Animal Protection Bill—with an inkprint of his paw. In 1973, he received the Patsy Award (given to the Picture Animal Top Star of the Year), the animal equivalent of the Oscar. He was featured in Time magazine and appeared in major motion pictures like *The Long Goodbye* and *Shamus*.

He also "wrote" two books and was the subject of *Morris: An Intimate Biography* by Mary Daniels. During his heyday, he and Martwick traveled about 200,000 miles together.

Morris passed away in 1978, at the age of nineteen. He was buried in Martwick's garden in Chicago. But that was not the end of the Morris legacy. Morris II, also discovered by Martwick, took up the mantle and held the job for fifteen years before retiring. Morris II died in 1997.

Morris III had a brief career before being replaced by Morris IV, who lives with his trainer, Rose Ordile, in Los Angeles. To most cat lovers, there is no Morris like the original, but the current Morris has something his forebear (fore-cat?) could not imagine: a Facebook page.

Did You Know?

Morris the Cat (the second Morris) ran for President of the United States in 1988. One poll revealed that Morris had higher name recognition than any other candidate but George H.W. Bush, who won the election. More recently, Morris IV has been the centerpiece of the Million Cat Rescue, an effort to find homes for homeless cats.

From generation to generation
we will proclaim your praise.

PSALM 79:13

80

CHINA VERSUS EGYPT VERSUS . . . CYPRUS?

It is commonly believed that the ancient Egyptians were the first to domesticate cats, as we have seen earlier in this book. However, as we have also learned, China is a contender for First Cat Civilization as well.

But if you're going to choose sides in this debate, you'll have to pick one of three, not two. According to Smithsonian.com, the Mediterranean island of Cyprus is the site of the grave of, perhaps, the oldest known pet cat. This grave dates back more than 9,500 years, predating early Egyptian art depicting house cats by a staggering 4,000 years. (An earlier dig on Cyprus revealed a cat's jawbone, dating back 8,000 years.)

It seems unlikely that humans would have brought wild cats to the island. As Desmond Morris notes in his *Catworld: A Feline Encyclopedia*, a "spitting, scratching, panic-stricken wild feline would have been the last kind of boat companion they would have wanted." Thus, the finding of a grave in which a cat had been intentionally buried with a human leads one to conclude that ancient cats, already on the island, were domesticated. Or, some already-domesticated cats took that ancient boat ride to Cyprus with their owners.

It can be fun to debate "Who were the first cat-lovers?" However, maybe it's better to just thank all of the contenders.

Did You Know?
The fierce Vikings took cats along on their ships, as the felines protected the warriors' food from mice and rats.

$\overline{\mathbf{O}\mathbf{O}}$

We love because he first loved us.

I JOHN 4:19

81

KE$HA SAYS, "CATS ROCK!"

When Ke$ha wears a cat-print outfit in concert, it's more than a fashion statement. The rock star, who was born Kesha Rose Sebert and grew up on welfare and food stamps, loves her cats—and animals in general. Her cats have their own sanctuary at home. "They have their own room," she explains. "They have their own couches. We have huge balls of yarn. I had them custom-made for my cats."

She has started her own "cat cult," which people can join if "they like to be cats or play with cats or play with cat toys." For more information, you can check out @KeshasCatCult on Twitter.

On a more serious note, Ke$ha is an outspoken opponent of product-testing on animals. She was named the Humane Society International's first global ambassador. She has starred in public-service ads for the organization's Be Cruelty Free campaign. Recently, she was honored with the Wyler Award by the United States' chapter of the Humane Society, noting her efforts to increase awareness of animal-related issues via the media.

"Advocating for animals is second nature to me," she explains. "My affinity with animals and the natural world inspires me and my music. I don't understand how anyone can justify abusing or exploiting animals. As long as it continues, I intend to keep talking about it."

Did You Know?

There are more than 500 million domestic cats in the world, with more than 40 recognized breeds.

Love always protects.

1 CORINTHIANS 13:7

IS YOUR CAT A SHOW-OFF?

The first formal cat show, just for pedigree cats, was held on July 17, 1871 at London's Crystal Palace. Organized by Harrison Weir, founder of the National Cat Club of the U.K., the show featured 160 exhibits. Today, cat shows are held worldwide, but they still mirror the "points of exhibition" established in the 1800s.

Of course, people have wanted to show off their cats for a long time. Less-formal "cat exhibitions" were held as far back as the 1500s. Most contemporary shows last two days. The shows feature anywhere from 200 to more than 1,000 cats. The criteria vary slightly by breed, but, in general, judges evaluate things like a cat's coat, balance, refinement, and coloring.

If you think you have a "show cat" in your midst, contact the Cat Fanciers Association or the Independent Cat Association, the two main governing bodies in the United States.

Did You Know?

The Governing Council of the Cat Fancy's Supreme Cat Show regularly draws more than 1,000 cat competitors.

You gave me life and showed me kindness,
and in your providence watched over my spirit.

JOB 10:12

TALK TO THE TAIL!

Surveys reveal that more than 95 percent of us talk to our cats. But how many of us listen? Or watch? Like humans, cats convey much with non-verbal communication. For example, if your cat is happy or feeling cocky, it will raise its tail like a flag. Fear, doubt, and uncertainty will lower that tail.

Further, a cat wagging or thumping its tail on the floor doesn't mean the same thing as a doggy tail-wag. For a cat, that wavy tail means trouble, not friendliness.

Is your cat's tail tip twitching a bit? That feline is concentrating hard—or perhaps experiencing a moment of indecision. (Perhaps, "Should I pounce on your stocking foot . . . or not?") And if your cat walks by you, carrying that tail high and proud, it's one way of saying, "Hi there! Nice to see you! It's a great day, isn't it?"

When a cat rolls over on its back, it might be soliciting a tummy-rub. Or, this might be a simple sign of trust and friendship. If you decide to reward this gesture with a tummy-petting session, don't worry about "How long do I need to keep this up." Your cat will let you know.

Speaking of Cats . . .

"Although your cat commands an impressive vocal repertoire, he communicates most eloquently through versatile body language. Every part of the body . . . even overall body posture speaks volumes about a cat's mood, intent, and current preoccupation."

Wendy Christensen

He performs signs and wonders
in the heavens and on the earth.

DANIEL 6:27

84

QUOTH THE CAT . . .

In his stories, like the classic "The Black Cat," author Edgar Allan Poe often used cats as the symbol of something sinister. In real life, the author of all things spooky loved cats. In fact, his tortoise-shell feline Catterina was the inspiration for "The Black Cat."

When Poe's wife, Virginia, was dying of tuberculosis (in 1847), Catterina would curl up in bed with her to provide warmth and comfort.

Two years later, the forty-year-old author passed away as well. To this day, no one is sure how or why. However, his last words were, "Lord, help my poor soul."

Upon hearing of the author's demise, Poe's mother-in-law went to check on Catterina. She found that the beloved cat had also passed away.

Speaking of Cats . . .

"I wish I could write as mysterious as a cat."

Edgar Allan Poe

∞

I said to myself, "Relax and rest. GOD has showered you with blessings. Soul, you've been rescued from death. . . .

PSALM 116:7-8

85

LUCKY LINDY'S CAT

Charles Lindbergh had a fearless love for flying. He was a stunt-flyer at barely twenty years old—wing-walking and parachuting from death-defying heights—to the delight of crowds. He made more than two hundred flights before he enrolled in flight school for his first technical training. By the time he was twenty-five, he was an expert pilot, arguably the best in the world.

Lindbergh also loved cats, especially his kitten, Patsy, who accompanied the legendary pilot on test flights of his brand-new Ryan monoplane, dubbed the *Spirit of St. Louis*. However, Lindbergh left Patsy behind when he made the legendary trans-continental flight from New York to Paris. Lindbergh was willing to risk his own life, but not his cat's. As he explained, "It's too dangerous a journey to risk the cat's life."

Lindbergh completed his flight in thirty-three and a half hours, battling winds, fog, and fatigue. (By the time he completed his flight, he had endured more than fifty-five hours without sleep.) To the delight of the world, including Patsy, he landed safely. One can imagine him curling up with Patsy for a long cat-nap when he returned home. A Spanish stamp commemorating the flight depicts Patsy, looking on anxiously, as her owner takes off in the *Spirit of St. Louis*.

Did You Know?

The first cat in space was the French feline Felicette, nicknamed Astrocat. Felicette rocketed into outer space in 1963. The cat was hooked up to sensors to monitor her vital signs and neurological activity. Thankfully, Felicette survived the trip.

Be glad, good people! Fly to GOD!
Good-hearted people, make praise your habit.

PSALM 64:10 MSG

86

THE SILENT MEOW

There are few cat behaviors more endearing than that sweet, open-mouthed silent meow. It's hard to resist. It's as if your cat is telling you, "I'm so hungry that I'm speechless!" or "I missed you so much that I have no words to express it!"

But is the silent meow truly silent? To us humans, perhaps, but not to other cats. As we have learned elsewhere in this book, cats can detect sounds at much higher frequencies than we can—around 65 kilohertz or higher, compared to our limit of about 20 kilohertz.

So, your cat's supposedly silent plea is just an ordinary meow. It's simply pitched *above* your auditory range. Why does a cat keep using this humanly unhearable sound? Probably because it has discovered just how effectively it gets a cat exactly what it wants.

Did You Know?

Cats who really, really want to be fed will mimic a human baby's cries. A savvy cat will broadcast an urgent, baby-like cry or meowing sound at nearly the same auditory frequency as a hungry infant.

"In my distress I called to the LORD;
I called out to my God. From his temple
he heard my voice; my cry came to his ears.

2 SAMUEL 22:7

87

FRANCO LOVES FELINES

As someone who defies easy categorization, it's not surprising that James Franco is a cat guy. The actor, filmmaker, author, and doctoral student was raised as a cat person. "I had cats when I was a kid," he explains, "and that's what I'm used to. I really don't know how to take care of a dog, but I think I'm pretty good with cats." He has been known to show up for formal black-tie events with cat hair on his clothes. "You've seen some of their hair," he told reporters at one New York high-ticket gala.

As a guy who was once enrolled in three creative-writing graduate programs at once, it's not surprising that Franco names his cats after literary characters. "Sammy is named after Sammy Glick from *What Makes Sammy Run*," he says. "Zelda is named after Zelda Fitzgerald. Two other cats, which my brother, Dave, stole from me, are Harry, after Harry Angstrum from the Rabbit novels, and Arturo is named after Arturo Bandini from the John Fante novels."

Franco soon replenished the "cat deficit" caused by his brother. After wrapping up work on the movie *Homefront*, Franco adopted Lux and Max, a cat who appeared in the film— and that cat's stunt double!

Speaking of Cats . . .

"My three cats are so full of energy that
I named them Caffeine, Guarana, and Taurine."

Marcia Edwards

"You are welcome to stay at my house.
Let me give you anything you need."

JUDGES 19:20 NCV

88

A DOG—LIKE CAT?

his book has addressed the friendly rivalry between cat
lovers and dog lovers. Of course, most animal lovers adore
both the canine and the feline. But many cat owners sometimes
confess, "Why can't my cat be more like a dog?"

If you've ever echoed this sentiment, consider the Birman
cat, perhaps the world's most dog-like cat. Legend has it that
the Birmans are descended from the sacred temple cats of
Burma. (Another theory is that they are a simple cross-breed
of the Siamese and the Longhair. Whatever the case, Birmans
are agreeable cats with long and silky coats, marked by their

distinctive white "gloves" (paws). They are clever and not as demanding or vocal as a Siamese or Burmese.

Birmans are friendly, out-going, and even-tempered. They adopt well to change—a rare trait for cats—who love routine and predictability. Birmans will come to you when called and might even bound to the doorway to greet you after a long day at work, just as a dog would.

So, the next time someone tells you, "Why can't cats be more like dogs?" think of the Birman and answer, "They can."

Incidentally, the Birman breed was first recognized in France in 1925. However, in the chaos of World War II, the breed almost became extinct. At one point, there were only two surviving Birmans in the world. They survived, and Birmans were first officially recognized as a purebred breed in the UK in 1966. America recognized the breed one year later.

Did You Know?

How did Birmans get those distinctive white paws? According to legend, the Birmans descend from the sacred Burmese temple cats. These cats could sense when a priest was dying. A temple cat would approach a dying priest and put its paws on him, to offer love and support during those final hours. When the priest died, the cat's paws turned white.

A true friend is always loyal. . . .

PROVERBS 17:17 TLB

THE BLESSING OF BARNEY

For more than twenty years, mourners at Saint Sampson's Cemetery in Guernsey, England, were comforted by a cat. Barney, a ginger tabby, would roam the cemetery grounds, gracing grieving people with his presence. According the Reverend Timothy Dack, "Whenever I was taking a funeral up there, families were so happy to see Barney milling around. The mourners would see him, and it would bring them a lot of joy. I think the presence of Barney brought a lot of comfort to so many people."

Barney originally lived with his owners next door to the cemetery. However, after the family moved, Barney kept returning to the cemetery grounds, where he seemed to have an innate sense of an adult or child who needed comforting. His gracious owners allowed him to be re-homed at Saint Sampson's, where he was cared for by cemetery employees.

One of the employees, Alan Curzon, noted, "When relatives and friends have suffered the awful loss of someone close to them and go to visit a cemetery, they are not in the best frame of mind. But Barney was always there to cheer them up. For those who entered the cemetery with a heavy heart, he lightened up the experience for them. When people walked through the gates, he often came up to them and brushed against them. There was not a bad bone in his body."

When Barney passed away in early 2016, he was laid to

rest at Saint Sampson's. A plaque on the cemetery wall and a "memorial bench" stand as tributes. Upon Barney's passing, dozens of people expressed their condolences and gratitude on social media. Sue Falla, whose daughter is buried at the cemetery, said, "I always felt my young daughter was never alone when he was there. I'm really going to miss you, Barney."

> *Did You Know?*
> Hallmark Cards Inc. began creating sympathy cards for pets in the 1920s.

∞

The Lamb on the Throne will shepherd them,
will lead them to spring waters of Life. And God will
wipe every last tear from their eyes.

REVELATION 7:17 MSG

90

YOUR FELINE FAVORS CLASSICAL MUSIC (PROBABLY)

Have you ever wondered what kind of music cats prefer? Hard rock? Classic rock? Country? Dub-step? Maybe some Taylor Swift, as she is, perhaps, the biggest cat lover in all of popular music

According to a published study in the *Journal of Feline Medicine and Surgery*, the answer is classical music. To arrive at this conclusion, a group of Portuguese veterinarians placed headphones on a dozen female cats who were being spayed. During the procedure, the cats listened to two minutes each of three different kinds of music. Their breathing rate and pupil diameter offered insight into their responses. "While the cats were listening to classical music," the study concluded, "their heart rates were slow, and their pupils were small, indicating they were relaxed. [The music of] AC/DC, on the other hand, had exactly the opposite effect, and the pop song [by Natalie Imbruglia] fell somewhere in between."

While this study might seem frivolous, or the product of some vets with too much idle time, it provides helpful information. If classical music can calm cats during various surgical procedures, the study concludes, veterinarians can use lower doses of anesthesia. And that will make operations safer for cats everywhere.

By the way, if you're curious which classical piece was used in the study, it was Barber's "Adagio for Strings (Opus 11)." Give it a try the next time you have a nervous cat on your hands.

Speaking of Cats . . .

"Never wear anything that panics the cat."
P.J. O'Rourke

Sing and make music from your heart to the Lord. . . .

EPHESIANS 5:19

91

THE MYSTERY OF THE PURR

We all know that cats purr when they are content and feeling loved. But did you know that cats also purr when they're sick, nursing, wounded, or stressed out? Some female cats purr rhythmically while they give birth.

So, why do cats purr? Scientists and veterinarians have many theories, but no sure answers. "Cats purr during both inhalation and exhalation, with a consistent pattern and frequency between 25 and 150 hertz," says Leslie Lyons, an assistant professor at the School of Veterinary Medicine at the University of California, Davis. "Various investigators have shown that sound frequencies in this range improve bone density and promote healing. Because cats have adapted to conserve energy via long periods of rest and sleep, it is possible that purring is a low-energy mechanism that stimulates muscles and bones without a lot of energy."

If you didn't completely understand those last two sentences, don't fret. It's another way of saying, "We're not sure."

Other veterinarians postulate that cats use purring to communicate, and as a source of coping and self-healing—an emotional outlet of sorts. The Humane Society notes, "A cat who is profoundly anything—content, happy, furious, in pain—purrs. The purr indicates an overflow of any emotion."

Here's one thing most everyone does agree on: Purring, while something of a mystery as far as the cat is concerned, is very good for humans. Stroking a purring cat can lower your blood pressure and your pulse rate. It will also enhance your sense of peace and well-being. Science or not, any cat owner will attest to the truth of "purr therapy."

Did You Know?

President Jimmy Carter and his family loved their cat, MistyMalarky Ying Yang, a sealpoint Siamese. In the White House, Misty could often be found curled up and purring in her favorite spot, First Daughter Amy Carter's doll house.

But godliness with contentment is great gain.

1 TIMOTHY 6:6

92

TIDY DRINKERS

Anyone who owns both cats and dogs can attest to the differing mess levels around a cat's and a dog's water bowl. The reason that cats are such tidy drinkers is that they drink differently than dogs. A dog will dip its tongue into the water, like a ladle. And we know what happens when liquid sloshes around in a ladle. Conversely, a cat touches only the surface of its tongue to the water. According to MIT News, "The smooth tip of the tongue barely touches the surface of the liquid before the cat draws its tongue back up. As it does so, a column of liquid forms between the moving tongue and the liquid's surface. The cat then closes its mouth, pinching off the top of the column for a nice drink, while keeping its chin dry."

This technique produces "liquid adhesion," meaning that water sticks to the cat's tongue. And the cat draws back its tongue so quickly that inertia (the tendency of the liquid to continue to follow the movement of the tongue) overcomes the gravity that might otherwise pull the water back down toward the bowl—or the floor. Then the cat snaps its mouth shut before the water can overcome the inertia and escape.

The bottom line: Cats are neater drinkers than dogs. But science, not social refinement or better manners, is the reason.

Did You Know?
Despite the enduring image of a cat drinking a bowl of cream or milk, most cats are lactose intolerant.

My soul thirsts for God, for the living God.

PSALM 42:2

93

A FOSTER PARENT FOR CATS

Not everyone has the schedule or the space to be a long-term cat owner. But there other options. Case in point: actor Jesse Eisenberg. The star of movies like *The Social Network* and *The End of the Tour* is a foster parent for cats. "I have two cats now," he said in a recent interview, "and I'm on a list where they can deliver them to the house. To be a foster parent for cats is, basically, to have tenants coming in and out. I have a lot of cats, a lot of cat food, a lot of litter—and nothing else in the apartment."

When you foster, you agree to take a homeless cat into your home and give him or her love, care, and sustenance, either for a predetermined time period or until the cat is adopted.

Eisenberg notes, "The more movies I do, the more guilty I feel—and the more cats I feel the need to get to alleviate the guilt from doing the movies. And then if a movie is popular, God forbid, then I have to get even more cats. If my cat Mr. Trunkles is any indication, cats are the greatest species on Earth."

If you are interested in fostering a cat, contact your local chapter of an animal-rescue group or a nearby animal shelter.

Speaking of Cats . . .

"My life is basically just feeding and cleaning cats.
And then I get to be the Sexiest Geek Alive.
It's a real blast."

Jesse Eisenberg

So look me in the eye and show kindness,
give your servant the strength to go on. . . .

PSALM 86:16 MSG

94

SO HARD TO SAY GOODBYE

Typically, a house cat lives about twenty years, the human equivalent of ninety-six. (The oldest cat on record was Crème Puff, from Austin, TX, who passed away three days after her thirty-eighth birthday. That's like a human living to the age of 182.)

Whenever it happens, saying goodbye to a beloved pet is heart-wrenching. In a survey of 1,300 cat and dog lovers, researchers found that half said losing their cat or dog was as heartbreaking as losing a close relative like an aunt, uncle, or grandparent. A third went even further, comparing a pet death to the death of a parent, sibling, or spouse.

Pet lovers noted that they mourn their pets for years. More than half of respondents said that their grief for their cat or dog "never goes away."

Writer Amy Sedaris spoke for many pet lovers when she said, "Sometimes losing a pet is more painful than losing a human because in the case of the pet, you were not pretending to love it."

Speaking of Pets . . .

"If there is a heaven, it's certain our animals
are to be there. Their lives become so interwoven
with our own that it would take more than
an archangel to detangle them."

Pam Brown

Blessed are those who mourn,
for they will be comforted.

MATTHEW 5:4

95

THE QUEEN OF
THE "CRAZY CAT LADIES?"

The term "crazy cat lady" isn't an insult to pop star Taylor Swift. It's a moniker she proudly owns. Just try to find one of her social-media posts that *doesn't* include one of her cats, Dr. Meredith Grey and Detective Olivia Benson. Neither of the cats holds an advanced degree or law-enforcement rank. Ms. Swift's felines are named after favorite TV characters from *Grey's Anatomy* and *Law & Order: SVU*, respectively.

One of Swift's Instagram videos shows Detective Olivia Benson frolicking with Mariska Hargitay, the actress who plays the human iteration of the character.

Both cats fly in private jets with their owner and seem to be as comfortable in front of a camera as their owner. Right now, Swift's is a two-cat household, but stay tuned. "It's a daily struggle not to buy more cats," she confesses.

Speaking of Cats . . .

"All I think about are metaphors and cats."

Taylor Swift

He sends his command to the earth;
his word runs swiftly.

PSALM 147:15

96

THE RIGHT PEDIGREE

The microblogging platform/social networking site Tumblr recently ran a meme that reflects the breed-centric tendencies (or lack thereof) of dog and cat people:

Dog person: "We have a purebred border collie with a Bernese twist."

Cat person: "This is Rita. We love her. She's orange."

However, today's cat owners are becoming more informed about pedigreed cats and how they can be wonderful pets, in the right home.

For example, if you want an easy-going and relatively quiet cat that is good with children, a Manx, Snowshoe, American shorthair, or Norwegian forest cat is a good choice. (American shorthairs were bred for hunting, so they are also great mousers.)

On the other hand, breeds like Burmese and Siamese are people-lovers, but they can be demanding. Birmans, Russian blues, and Bombays are mellow "lap cats," while Abyssians and Somalis are high-energy athletes who love to play and climb and explore. Abyssinians are sometimes called the World's Smartest Kitties, but, because they are rather shy around strangers (both human and feline), they are not the best show cats.

If you just cannot get enough cat-grooming, a Himalayan or Persian might be just the ticket for you.

For more information on a breed that might be a perfect

fit for your home, talk with a veterinarian, or you can research specific breeds on the Internet.

> *Did You Know?*
> The American shorthair breed first came to America on the *Mayflower*.

Seek good . . . that you may live.
Then the LORD God Almighty
will be with you. . . .

AMOS 5:14

97

CAT FIGHT!

Not all feline battle royals are created equal. Some cat conflicts that seem serious at first glance turn out to be nothing but a game. Littermates, especially when they are very young, often engage in vigorous grappling matches, for exercise and fun.

Savvy cat owners learn to distinguish a "play fight" from a no-claws-barred cat throw-down. Here are some signs to look for:

1. Does the cats' body language indicate true aggression or terror?
2. Are the cats' claws fully extended and battle-ready?
3. Are tufts of fur flying as a result of the scuffle?
4. Are one or more combatants screaming, yowling, or emitting a deep, guttural sound?

If you recognize any of the above signs, there's a good chance you have a real fight on your hands, and a cat could be in danger of a serious injury. However, don't try to break up a cat fight by picking up and removing one of the combatants. You could end up being scratched or bitten yourself. Instead, yell and sharply, smack your hands together, or whistle loudly. This might halt the battle—and cause at least one of the cats to escape to a neutral corner.

If the above technique isn't sufficient, toss a soft pillow into the fray, or give the angry cats a squirt of water. After a fight is broken up, keep the battling cats apart for at least a few hours. They need time to calm down. Then, don't let them interact without your careful supervision. Soon, you will have a good idea as to whether or not the battle will be rejoined.

Don't try to punish cats for overly aggressive behavior. This will serve only to confuse or annoy them. If you find that you have two or more perennially contentious cats on your hands, you might need to visit the vet. A cat (or cats) might need medication and a behavior-modification program. Don't worry about turning a kittie into a catatonic druggie. There are several non-tranquilizing medications that soothe aggressive behavior and smooth inter-cat relationships. Once peace is restored, a cat can be weaned off the meds.

Speaking of Cats . . .
"No matter how much cats fight,
there always seem to be plenty of kittens."
Abraham Lincoln

Blessed are the peacemakers,
for they will be called children of God.

MATTHEW 5:9

CATS ON BROADWAY

"Destiny waits in the hand of God,
not in the hands of statesmen."

T. S. Eliot

One has to marvel at how the world of literature and theater would be different if T. S. Eliot were not a cat lover. The acclaimed poet helped reshape modern literature, with verses sometimes whimsical and sometimes deeply serious and spiritual. He penned rhymes and free verse—although he was quick to point out, "No verse is free for the man who wants to do a good job."

Eliot received the Nobel Prize for literature in 1948, at the age of sixty. Works like *The Love Song of J. Alfred Prufrock* and *The Waste Land*, which explored the spiritual bankruptcy Eliot saw in the modern world, are among his most critically acclaimed works. But nothing has affected popular culture as much as his 1939 collection, *Old Possum's Book of Practical Cats*, which he dedicated to his godchildren.

This lesser-known book was adopted by Andrew Lloyd Webber for a musical titled, simply, *Cats*, featuring felines with markedly different personalities and life stories, just as the cats Eliot had known and loved during his life.

Because Eliot wrote such wonderful poetry, Webber did not have to write any song lyrics for the musical. He simply set Eliot's verses to music. *Cats* opened in 1981, won the Best Musical Tony Award in 1983, and ran until the year 2000—"retiring" as the world's longest-running musical. Audiences in twenty-six countries saw it. The musical's signature song, "Memory," has been recorded by more than 150 artists, from Barbra Streisand to Barry Manilow to Judy Collins.

The musical introduced to the world several "cat stars" from some of Eliot's unpublished drafts of *Old Possum's Book of Practical Cats*. One of these was Grizabella the Glamour Cat, whom Eliot edited from his final draft because he thought the character and her storyline were "too sad for children." However, Eliot's widow, Valerie, gave Webber several unpublished poems, including "Grizabella the Glamour Cat." Today, it's hard to imagine the musical without Grizabella. And it's hard to imagine a world without *Cats*. Or cats.

Speaking of Cats . . .

"You've read of several kinds of Cat,
And my opinion now is that
You should need no interpreter
To understand their character.
You now have learned enough to see
That Cats are much like you and me."

T.S. Eliot
(from "Old Possum's Book of Practical Cats")

The heavens declare the glory of God;
the skies proclaim the work of his hands.

PSALM 19:1

99

A TALE OF TWO (OR MORE) KITTIES

*"I know that, but for the mercy of God,
I might easily have been, for any care
that was taken of me, a little robber
or a vagabond."*

Charles Dickens

What greater gift than the love of a cat?" wrote literary giant Charles Dickens. Dickens's cats were his companions during his long hours of longhand writing of books like *A Tale of Two Cities*, *Great Expectations*, and *David Copperfield*. However, when the felines needed some attention, they would impose a work break on their owner by snuffing the flame on his desk candle with a deft flick of a paw.

Dickens didn't mind the interruption one bit. His favorite cat was named Bob. When Bob, who was deaf, passed away in 1862, Dickens was so distraught that he had the feline's paw stuffed and mounted onto an ivory letter opener. He had the opener engraved with the words, "C.D., In memory of Bob, 1862." He wanted a constant reminder of his dearest feline friend. That letter opener is now on display at the Berg Collection of English and American Literature at the New York Public Library.

> *Speaking of Cats . . .*
>
> "One loyal cat is worth a truckload of in-laws."
>
> *Taylor Morgan*

For the LORD your God is a merciful God....

DEUTERONOMY 4:31

100

CATS ARE FAMILY

Many of us cat lovers have fond memories of our childhood cats, and we'd like to pass on this shared experience to our children. However, pet ownership is more than a family tradition. Owning a cat (or two) can help a child learn love, respect, responsibility, and empathy.

By caring for a pet, a child gains a sense of accomplishment and personal competence. As responsible pet owners know, the way we care for our cats, dogs, etc., has real-life consequences. Kids can see the fruits of their labor in a happy, healthy cat. Further, they learn to value the idiosyncrasies, needs, and the very lives of another creature who is sharing their living space.

Even a toddler can learn to handle the family cat gently, appreciating the cat's fragility, but also its power. As a kid grows older, he or she can be involved in feeding, grooming, administering medication, or helping with a trip to the vet. In turn, kids find that they have a feline friend who will be loyal to them through thick and thin—or from algebra tests to broken hearts.

And, of course, owning a cat helps us adults set a good example, as we model patience and self-control and keep up with trends in nutrition, animal care, and veterinary medicine.

Learning about and caring for cats can be a lifelong family labor of love. If done well, your children will carry on this sacred trust with their own families someday—with some very blessed cats.

Speaking of Cats . . .

"One small cat changes coming home to an empty house to coming home."

Pam Brown

I kneel before the Father,
from whom every
family in heaven and on earth
derives its name.

EPHESIANS 3:14-15

LOOKING FOR KITTY CONVICTS

If California-based cartoonist Matthew Inman has his way, every housecat will sport an orange collar emblazoned with its name and phone number. That way, if a cat gets loose or lost, the collar will be a signal, shouting "Help me!" Inman has dubbed his collar campaign the Kitty Convict Project. Its goal: To increase the percentage of missing cats reunited with their owners.

As Inman notes, when dogs are loose, they are often picked up, on the assumption that they are lost. When people see a roaming cat, they often assume it is allowed to explore, or that it's feral.

According to the ASPCA, 15 percent of pet owners have lost their cat or dog. However, while 93 percent of lost dogs are recovered, the percentage drops to 74 for cats. Further, ASPCA research indicates that while 80 percent of pet owners say it is important to place ID tags on their pets, only 30 percent actually provide them. "Overall use of collar ID tags is lower for cats than dogs," explains Dr. Emily Weiss, vice president of ASPCA shelter research and development. "The likelihood of your being reunited is lower if it's a cat. People wait longer to look, and about 25 percent don't come home."

Inman thinks he can change things. He says he's already sold thousands of his orange Kitty Convict collars. (They are available

on Amazon.com for $14.) The collars are custom-stitched with
the cat's name and a contact phone number. "We want to change
what people see when they see a cat," Inman says.

For cats, it seems, orange is the new "safe."

Did You Know?

Cartoonist Matthew Inman's Kitty Convict Project has
been subsidized by the $9 million he raised on the
crowd-funding site Kickstarter for his gaming app
"Exploding Kittens," which is just a card game that
doesn't involve harming felines in any way. "It was
a horrible name for a game," Inman confesses. "My
collar project is cat atonement, or 'catonement.'"

"Ask, and you will be given what you ask for.
Seek, and you will find.
Knock, and the door will be opened."

MATTHEW 7:7 TLB

"God spoke: "Earth, generate life!
Every sort and kind:
cattle and reptiles and wild animals—
all kinds" And there it was:
wild animals of every kind . . .
God saw that it was good."

GENESIS 1:24-25 MSG

About the Author

TODD HAFER is an award-winning writer whose fifty-plus books have sold more than two million copies. His teen/young adult novel *Bad Idea* was a Christy Awards finalist and its sequel, *From Bad to Worse*, was named one of the top ten books of the year by Christian Fiction Reviews. *Bad Idea* is currently being made into a feature-length film. His book *Life Saver: The Ultimate Devotional Handbook for Teens* was an ECPA book of the year finalist. Todd lives on the plains of eastern Kansas with his children, a wayward rescue dog (who hopes to make cat-befriending an Olympic sport), and his very patient wife. For more about Todd, visit HaferBrothers.com.

Partial Bibliography

- *The Complete Cat Book* by Paddy Cutts, Hermes House, 2001.
- *The New Cat Handbook* by Ulrike Muller, Barron's Educational Series, 1984.
- *Complete Guide to Cat Care*, by Wendy Christensen and the Staff of the Humane Society of the United States. St. Martin's Press, 2002.
- *Cat Speak by Bash Dibra*, G.P. Putnam's Sons, 2001.
- *One Summer: America 1927*, by Bill Bryson, Anchor Books, 2013.
- *The Traverse City News-Record*, February 11, 2016 edition.
- *Fun Facts for Hunters* by Todd Hafer, Barbour & Company, 2010.
- *Everything Romance: A Celebration of Love for Couples*, by Todd Hafer, WaterBrook/Random House, 2011.

Notes

....
....
....
....
....
....
....
....
....
....
....
....
....
....
....
....
....
....
....
....
....
....
....

Notes

....
....
....
....
....
....
....
....
....
....
....
....
....
....
....
....
....
....
....
....
....
....
....
....
....

Notes

Notes

....
....
....
....
....
....
....
....
....
....
....
....
....
....
....
....
....
....
....
....
....
....
....